Recollections of Oxenholme

by

W. L. Harris

as related to

Edward Talbot

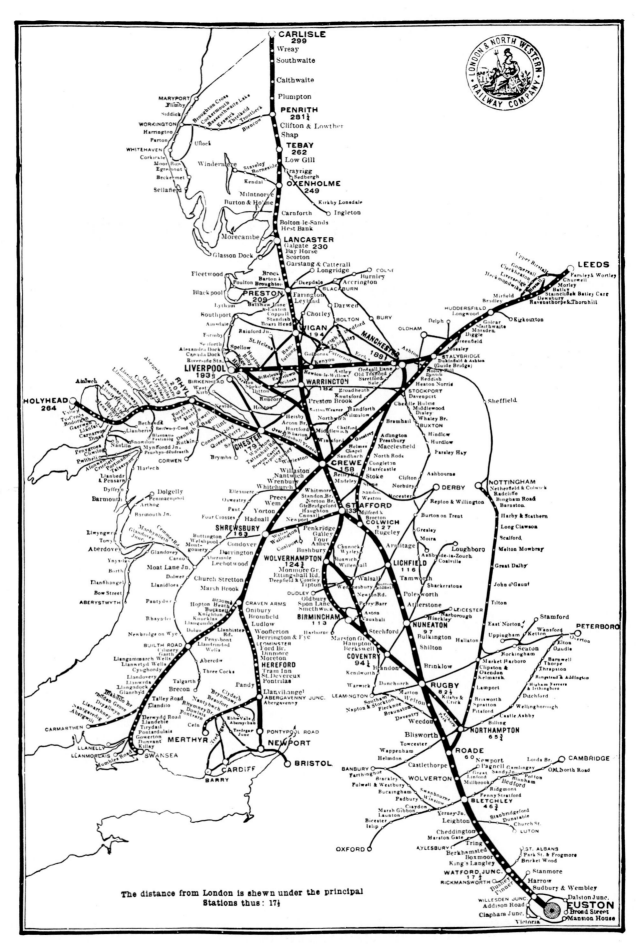

Map of the LNWR taken from the 1907 timetable.

Preface and Acknowledgements

When my book *An Illustrated History of LNWR Engines* was published, I received a number of letters from enthusiasts. Among them was one from W. L. Harris, who I was soon to discover had made a lifelong study of LNWR engines. He is now over ninety years of age, having been born in 1900, and once counted among his friends the late Charles Williams of Crewe, the noted authority on the LNWR and its locomotives, as well as many other enthusiasts of that period.

After a time, I was invited to visit him at his home and was fascinated by his recollections of the great years of the LNWR when the 'George the Fifths' were new on the line over Shap, of the enginemen and railway operations around Oxenholme, and of the unusual workings during the First World War, particularly the special Admiralty coal trains. I soon realised that they would be of great interest to other enthusiasts also and were worth writing up in full.

This book is the result. In some respects the language has changed slightly since he grew up but so far as possible the text is a faithful record of his own words as he recounted his recollections to me. Similarly I have retained his terminology in reference to the LNWR, as for example in the names of the various engine classes and in his description of the carriage livery, 'chocolate and cream'. Whereas present-day enthusiasts associate that phrase with the Great Western Railway, in the pre-grouping era it was commonly taken as referring to the LNWR whose carriages were a dark chocolate and a very pale cream, almost white.

Since that first invitation I have visited 'John' and his charming wife Ada on numerous occasions and have greatly enjoyed and appreciated their kind hospitality. I hope readers will find his recollections as fascinating as I have and will obtain as much pleasure from them as I have had in putting them on record.

Finally, I should like to thank all those who have helped in any way with the production of this book, in particular F. W. Shuttleworth for printing some of the pictures and providing others, and Richard D. Foster for the maps. The photographs are individually credited except for those by unknown photographers from my own collection. W. L. Harris himself took photographs and it is fortunate that some are able to be included.

Edward Talbot
Stafford
1993

Introduction

My interest in the railway all began in the summer of 1911 when I was eleven years old, having been born in 1900. With my brother Jim I attended the Grammar School in Kendal, which is situated on the southern outskirts of the town about a mile and a quarter from Oxenholme. Jim is eighteen months younger than I am and so was in a lower class in school. At that time he used to finish at four o'clock whereas I came out at four fifteen. So I used to arrive home later than he did and we often never saw each other until we both got home.

One day Jim was late home. When he came in he said he had been to Oxenholme station with a boy called Slater who was making a list of the names and numbers of the engines. I thought that might be interesting and so the next day I went with them to see what it was all about. My interest was immediate and though my brother's interest soon faded, mine never has to this day and I can still recall those times quite clearly. Thanks to a wonderful memory and copious records the information I gathered is still there.

The first engine I saw was No. 941 *Blenkinsop* which was stationed at Oxenholme and which I later discovered was a 'Big Jumbo'. The second was the 'Precursor' 374 *Empress*. It had recently been through the works at Crewe and had been repainted before being sent to Oxenholme. It was always well cleaned and polished and was a wonderful sight in the summer sunshine. The driver and fireman were very friendly and told me a lot about the different classes of engines.

The 'Precursor' *Empress,* which was the second LNWR engine I saw.

Roger Carpenter collection

The magnificent condition in which the whole of the LNWR was maintained in the years immediately before the First World War is well shown in this classic view of the down 2pm 'Corridor' near Kenton about 1913. The engine is 'Prince of Wales' class 4-6-0 No. 979 *W. M. Thackeray,* which will work the train as far as Crewe. After a two-hour break for a rest and a meal, the driver and fireman will return to London with the same engine on the corresponding up 'Corridor', which left Crewe at 7.32pm.

H. Gordon Tidey

'George the Fifth' No. 1059 *Lord Loch,* which was hauling the Royal Train when I saw it at Birklands Bridge. The photograph was taken at Manchester London Road about 1914.

W. H. Whitworth

Before the First World War

Oxenholme was a wonderful place then, for the years from 1911 to 1914 were the finest period ever of the London & North Western Railway. The passenger trains were a magnificent sight with their chocolate and cream coaches all kept in beautiful condition, and with their black engines all cleaned and polished, lined out in red, yellow and dove grey, and with the brasswork all polished up. The permanent way was superb and the operating and service were second to none. Moreover, the advent of the 'George the Fifth' class in 1910 had revolutionised the working of the express passenger trains, especially between Crewe and Carlisle. Whereas the 'Precursors' and 'Experiments' were regularly helped over the top of Shap with 360 tons, that went by the board completely when the 'George the Fifths' were introduced. They took nearly 400 tons over Shap without assistance. The highest recorded that I have seen was 390 tons.

A typical example of their haulage capacity occurred one day in 1911. One of the places where I used to go to watch trains was Birklands Bridge, about a mile north of Oxenholme station. It is adjacent to a big house called Birklands, from which of course it takes its name. This was the home of the Wakefield family, which was famous for its firm manufacturing lubricators, and to which the great rugby player W. W. Wakefield belonged. The bridge was built of blocks of the local limestone and the coping was quite wide. I used to sit on the end of this bridge and because it was a skew bridge I got a good side view of the trains as they passed.

When I got to the bridge on this particular occasion I noticed the platelayers were all standing along the line with green and red flags in their hands. One of them saw us on the bridge - Jim was with me - and came up and stood beside me. I said to him, 'What's happening, anyway?' 'Oh,' he said, 'the Royal Train's coming'. I think he came to see we did not do any damage to it!

The pilot engine came through first - it was a 'Big Jumbo', No. 1522 *Pitt* - and then came the Royal Train itself. It was hauled by only one engine, 'George the Fifth' No. 1059 *Lord Loch*, fully painted and lined, and the carriages were chocolate and cream, a really beautiful sight. The train was going north and presumably the royal passengers were going to Scotland for the grouse shooting. It was a big heavy train but it would go over Shap without assistance. Once it had gone the men disappeared again, back to their jobs on the line.

In fact, the 'George the Fifths' were so successful that they took the whole railway world by storm. Thanks to the use of a high-degree superheater, producing steam at up to 700°F, and piston valves that were very carefully designed and set, and driven indirectly by rocking levers, they were very powerful engines. Indeed they were so powerful that they astounded everybody. Cecil J. Allen writing in his monthly article in *The Railway Magazine* said it was absolutely astonishing that the engines seemed to have a ready store of latent power on which they could always call in an emergency.

A further twenty 'Georges' had been ordered for 1911 but because of the success of the design, this number was immediately doubled to forty and they were turned out as quickly as possible. In order to get them into traffic without delay they went straight into service from the erecting shop in shop grey. There was no coloured paint on them whatsoever. Even the background to the figures on the brass numberplates, which was usually painted red, was left just as cast. The nameplates were standard, the sunken letters being filled in with black stopping as usual.

In addition to the forty 'George the Fifth' class the first ten engines of the 'Prince of Wales' class which were also turned out in 1911 were put into traffic in the same condition, shop grey. These first ten 'Princes' were built without any trial and were superheated versions of the 'Experiment' class. All ten were stationed at Crewe when new and they did a wonderful job on the Crewe-Carlisle line. Two of the engines that were turned out in shop grey were called in quickly for painting. The 'George the Fifth' No. 1800 returned to the works immediately after trials to be prepared in its special livery as No. 5000 *Coronation* for the coronation of King George V and Queen Mary in June 1911; and the first of the 'Prince of Wales' class, No. 819 *Prince of Wales*, was called in for painting in February 1912. All the other forty-eight engines which were then in traffic in shop grey were finally painted and lined when they made their first visit to Crewe for general overhaul. This took place when they had run 120,000 miles or after they had been in service for fourteen months, whichever came first.

In 1913 a start was made on rebuilding the 'Precursors'. They were fitted with new superheated boilers, new cylinders and small bogie wheels exactly the same as on the 'Georges', so that as rebuilt they were exactly the same in power and appearance except that they retained their curved driving-wheel splashers instead of the straight ones of the 'Georges'.

On Saturday afternoon I usually managed to be on the platform at Oxenholme in time to see the 1.38pm from Preston. During the week this train was timed to pass Oxenholme at 2.25pm and arrive in Carlisle at 3.24pm. On Saturday it stopped at Oxenholme from 2.23 to 2.25pm but according to the working timetable it was still expected to be in Carlisle at the same time. The two minutes allowed for the stop at Oxenholme were only part of the total time lost through stopping, which also included the time required to slow down before the stop and to accelerate again after it, up the bank to Grayrigg.

The Royal Train taking King George V and Queen Mary from Euston to Crewe for their visit to the Works on 21st April 1913. The engines are both 'George the Fifths', No. 2663 *George the Fifth* and No. 5000 *Coronation.* When *Coronation* was new it was stationed at Crewe North shed and allocated to drivers J. Childs and W. Pascall; their names were painted inside the cab on the driver's side.   *W. Finch collection*

The following extract from the working timetable shows the timing of this train between Preston and Carlisle:

		Mon-Fri	Saturday
Preston	dep	1.38	1.38
Oxheys	pass	1.41	1.41
Lancaster	"	2.01	2.01
Carnforth	"	2.08	2.08
Oxenholme	"	2.25	2.23-5
Tebay	"	2.41	2.41
Shap Summit	"	2.52	2.52
Penrith	"	3.06	3.06
Carlisle	arr	3.24	3.24

This train was a Crewe North working and was usually hauled by a different engine every day. One Saturday in November 1913 the engine was 'Rebuilt Precursor' No. 2062 *Sunbeam*. By the way the driver started away from Oxenholme it was clear to me that he intended to keep time at all costs. By a very fortunate coincidence Cecil J. Allen was on the train and he timed the climb to Shap Summit in detail. The driver passed the summit in $24^{3}/_{4}$ minutes. The load of 265 tons gross was well within the capability of the engine; but even so this effort was surely a classic and illustrates how drivers always used to endeavour to keep time whatever the circumstances. Cecil J. Allen gave full details of the trip in *The Railway Magazine* in 1914 and O. S. Nock gave the timings in detail on page 90 of his book *The Precursor Family*.

Meanwhile, following its success on the 'George the Fifth' and 'Prince of Wales' classes, superheating was applied to goods engines. A series of 'Superheated Goods' was turned out in 1912 and they were a complete success too. Probably they were the best goods engines ever built in this country. They were exactly the same as the previous 'G' class, which were unsuperheated, but had the superheated boiler, $20^{1}/_{2}$in by 26in cylinders, and piston valves which were again driven indirectly by rocking levers.

By this time, 1912, I was able to more or less recognise every different class of engine by the sound of its exhaust. One morning in the Easter holidays in 1912 I was sitting on Birklands Bridge at about 11 o'clock when I heard a goods train coming through Oxenholme station without stopping. It was chittering away up the bank in a way I had never heard before so I knew it was something different but I could not think what it could be. As it came nearer and nearer I could see it looked like a 'G' or a 'D' but it had a much sharper exhaust. The number of the engine was 1426 and I found out afterwards that it was a superheated version of the 'D' and 'G' classes, one of the new 'Super Ds', and was one of those turned out in February 1912. On successive days I saw this same engine and also No. 1633, both of which I should imagine were shedded at Crewe South because I found out later that the train they were working was a through working from Crewe to Carlisle known as the 'Camden Goods'. They seemed to handle these trains quite easily, with no effort.

'Rebuilt Precursor' No. 2062 *Sunbeam,* which I saw at Oxenholme before it made the exceptional climb over Shap timed by Cecil J. Allen. It is seen here at Stockport soon after being rebuilt.

I remember another incident with a 'Super D', in August 1914 just about the time when the war broke out. It was a lovely summer's day, very hot, with no wind and everything still. I was sitting in the same place one afternoon, after the 3 o'clock expresses had passed, when I heard a 'Super D' coming long before it got to Oxenholme station. It came through the station without stopping, chittering away up the bank past me. It was one of the latest new engines which had been turned out in June and July, No. 2058, fully painted and lined and all cleaned and polished and shining – it looked wonderful. It went past me and under the bridge and under the next bridge and the next – there are three bridges quite close to each other – and I just sat there and listened to it and I was absolutely astonished how long the sound of its exhaust could be heard in the still afternoon. I am sure I could hear it until the engine disappeared into the deep rock cutting on the lower slopes of Benson Knot,

just before it got to Hay Fell signal box. Then I lost the sound altogether. It was amazing that I could hear it for what must have been all of four miles.

Eventually, in LMS days, the total number of 'Super Ds' in service, including conversions from other classes, reached 508. When the last few of them were withdrawn in December 1964, they were not only the last LNWR engines to survive but had also outlasted the LMS 'G3' class, which was only introduced in 1927.

After the first 'Claughton', No. 2222 *Sir Gilbert Claughton,* was completed in January 1913, it ran trial trips in shop grey and I was told it had been through to Carlisle in this condition. The first time I saw it was during the Easter holidays. It stopped at Oxenholme on either the 'Newspaper' 12.10-12.15pm or the 'Aberdeen', 4.32-4.34pm. It was in charge of Driver Ford of Crewe, who I knew by

One of the first batch of 'Claughtons' built in 1913, No. 21 *Duke of Sutherland,* in the spotless condition that was typical of LNWR engines before the First World War.

W. H. Whitworth

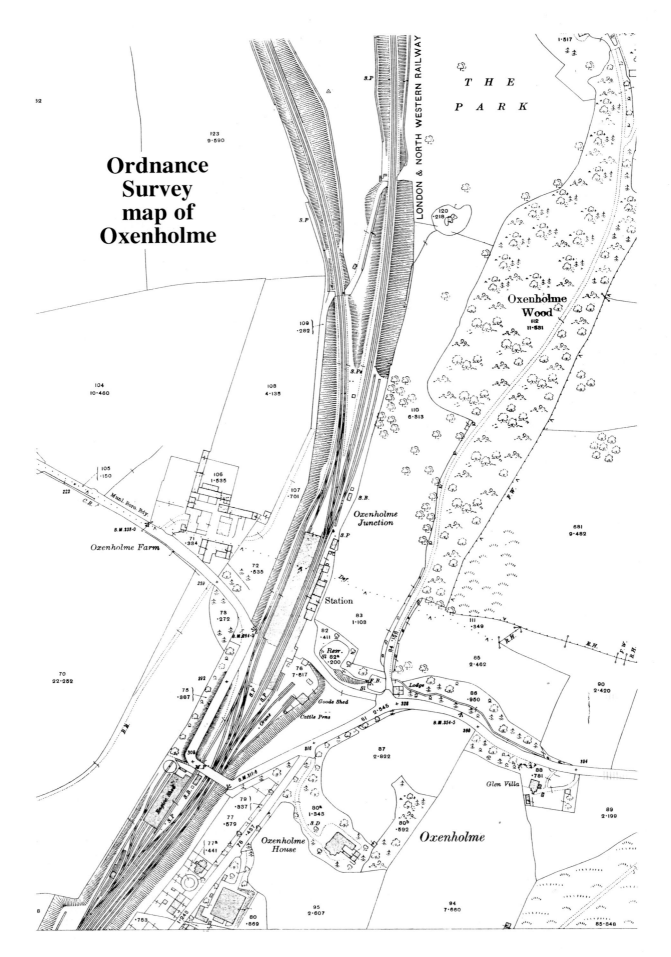

Ordnance
Survey
map of
Oxenholme

sight but had never spoken to. In fact, I never had any conversation with any 'foreign' drivers because the engines usually stopped off the end of the platform and were often blowing off anyway. The engine would be allocated to him and to another Crewe driver and their names would be painted in white on the inside of the cab side-sheet on the driver's side; it was not done in block capitals but in quite stylish handwriting. The inside of the cab of course was painted red ochre.

There was one occasion I remember when the 'Aberdeen', headed by 'George the Fifth' No. 2154 *William Siemens*, stopped well back in the platform because the track was set for the Windermere branch and the driver had to keep clear of the locking bar in front of the points. The roar of the safety valves within the confines of the station canopy was deafening but was nothing compared with the sound of the exhaust exploding when the driver opened up after being given the 'right away'. These are the sounds one remembers for ever.

Because I was often at the station, watching the trains, I got to know many of the Oxenholme drivers, and very fine men they were. They liked people to take an interest in what they were doing and I am proud to say I had a feeling of rapport with them. One evening I was standing on the main platform just before 7 o'clock. The 'Corridor' was due to pass at 7.08pm. It was a quiet evening. There was nobody about and I was by myself in the middle of the platform, out in the open at the south end. A 'Big Jumbo', No. 974 *Richard Cobden*, moved off the shed and came to rest where they always stopped when they were going to hook on to a passenger train, on the track outside the 'loop', which was what the two-way platform on the west side of the island platform was called. They used to stand there so that they could back straight down on to the front of the engine they were to assist, which would stop by the shed clear of the points. Fred Oates was the driver. I cannot remember exactly but I think he had never really spoken to me before. If he had, it was only a few words. But he had no sooner stopped than he called across to me 'We're hooking on the "Diner".' There was a note of great excitement in his voice, as much as to say 'It's a thrilling job this'. He meant the 'Corridor' and I signalled back 'OK' to acknowledge what he had told me. That was the sort of men they were. He was so thrilled to be hooking on the best express on the line that he had to tell somebody.

His engine that day, No. 974 *Richard Cobden,* went into Crewe in March 1919 with a cracked tyre but they cut it up. Over the years between 1911 and 1922 Oxenholme must have had about twenty 'Jumbos' in all. When sent to Crewe for overhaul, they were usually replaced by a different one.

Oxenholme Station

The station at Oxenholme covered quite a large area. South of the station was a quite extensive yard, at the south end of which was No. 1 signal box. It was a high box so that the signalman could see over the bridge which took the road from Kendal to Kirkby Lonsdale over the railway. It must have had about 25 levers.

This box controlled the entrance to the sidings on the down side. There were three of these; the first was known as 'the loop' and the others were Nos. 1 and 2. The box also controlled the outlet from the up loop. This was the only siding on the up side, presumably because it was easier to keep the traffic moving downhill than uphill. From No. 1 box, officially known as No. 1 South, to No. 2 was a distance of 644 yards. No. 2 box controlled the outlet from the down sidings, the entrance to the up loop, and the access to the engine shed. The shed stood behind the box and was a four-road shed complete with coaling stage and turntable. It was capable of dealing with about twenty engines. No. 2 box was also a high box, so that the signalman could see over the bridge south of the station which carried the Kendal to New Hutton road over the railway. It was the biggest box of the three and had about 60 levers.

From No. 2 box through the station to No. 3 box was 346 yards. No. 3 was officially known as No. 3 Junction, because it controlled the junction of the branch line to Kendal and Windermere. The tracks from the branch came straight across and joined the main line north of the platform ends and there was also a line to the bay platform.

The station itself consisted of one up platform on the east side, then the main line up and down tracks, then the island platform and then the single track on the west side of the island platform. This latter connected the main line from No. 2 box to the Kendal and Windermere branch and was used as a two-way platform. It was commonly referred to as the 'bay platform', although it was actually a through platform and not a 'bay' in the normal sense. In fact there were no bay platforms at all at Oxenholme. On the west side of the bay platform was a wall, which supported the overall roof and protected the station from the wind. Beyond the wall were two more tracks; the outer one enabled engines to pass from one end of the station to the other without using a platform road and the inner one was generally used for storing carriages.

At the south end of the up platform there was a dock for the gas-cylinder truck which supplied the station lighting system. From time to time it was sent to Carlisle to be refilled. As on other LNWR stations where trains ran through at speed, such as Penrith, Tebay, Carnforth and Lancaster, there was a bell with

The south end of Oxenholme station about 1900 with an up train hauled by a 'John Hick' class three-cylinder compound 2-2-2-2 awaiting departure; it is probably a stopping train from Carlisle to Crewe. The photograph was taken some years before I first went to Oxenholme but the layout and almost every other feature are the same.

View of the south end of Oxenholme station about 1912, taken from the window of No. 2 signal box looking over the 'Horse Shoe' bridge. Building materials are dumped at the end of the down platform in readiness for extending it southwards. *Bernard Matthews collection*

Two views of the south end of Oxenholme, taken from the overbridge by the shed on 5th April 1961. The signal box in the foreground, Oxenholme No. 2, was put in by the LMS in 1943 and replaced the LNWR boxes Nos. 2 and 3. The 'Black Five', No. 45108, is about to leave on an up parcels train.   *F. W. Shuttleworth*

a notice beneath it saying: 'The ringing of this bell indicates that a train is approaching that does not stop at this station'. It was actuated by the signalman as soon as he saw the train coming into view.

The Station Staff

So far as the general public was concerned, Oxenholme was little more than a wayside station where it was usually necessary to change trains for the branch to Windermere. This branch was eleven miles long and served Kendal and the intermediate villages of Burneside and Staveley. Between 1911 and 1920 the total station staff would not have been more than ten at the most.

The stationmaster was Mr Knight, a tall man who seemed to spend most of his time in his office, only appearing on the platform occasionally when one of the more important main-line trains was due. The ticket collector's surname was Nelson – I never knew his first name. He had a little wooden cabin on the down platform at the top of the subway. At some time in his railway service he had been in an accident, which caused him to lose his left hand, and he was then given the job of collecting the tickets. He had an artificial hand with imitation fingers between which he used to wedge the tickets so that he could punch them. There were two station foremen who worked alternate weeks on the morning and afternoon shifts. They were Alf Winder and Jim Mason. I am quite sure they both knew their jobs well but the signalmen preferred working with Alf because he could sort out the necessary shunting with fewer movements than Jim, thus making less work in the box.

There were two porters, the shunt porter and the lamp porter. One afternoon in the summer of 1913 I was on the down platform at the north end when the 'Aberdeen' arrived. This was the 10.30am from Euston and I assume it was so named because it eventually reached the Granite City. It was due to call at Oxenholme from 4.32 to 4.34pm. The engine was No. 650 *Lord Rathmore*, one of the ten new 'Claughtons' recently completed at Crewe. The vehicle next to the engine was a four-wheeled covered van and as I walked back down the platform I noticed the coupling between the van and the first coach was very slack. As I was standing looking at it, the porter shunter came down the platform – he had come from the up platform round the front of the engine. I pointed the coupling out to him but he said nothing and walked on, so I stood and waited to see what would happen. Sure enough, when the driver started away, the hook on the van snapped and the vacuum hose was torn in two. The engine and van stopped with a ten-yard gap between the first two vehicles. A spare hose was found but it was a good half hour before the train got away. During that time I kept out of the way.

I do not think many would envy the lamp porter. He was responsible for all the lamps in the whole of the station area. In the morning he would collect them all up, including those from the signals up the main Carlisle line and on the Windermere branch, put them on a barrow and take them to the lamp room. This was a small hut at the north end of the up platform. It was situated by itself away from the main station buildings because its store of lamp oil was a fire risk. There the lamp porter checked all the lamps, filled them with oil and trimmed the wicks if necessary. Then in the afternoon he had to take them all back to the various signals and dummies from which they had come.

This was a very important job, because it was vital that the lamps were working properly at night, and it had to be done every day of the year, in summer sunshine and winter snow. It was three quarters of a mile from the station to No. 3 box up distant signal and walking there and back twice a day made a total of three miles for that one signal alone; in deep snow, of course, it was very hard work indeed, especially carrying two full lamps. The biggest hazard, however, so far as this signal was concerned was climbing it in gale force winds. It was a very tall signal with two arms, one low down and the other right at the top, and it was situated in the middle of a very high embankment. It must have taken a great deal of courage to climb it in a howling gale; the ladder itself was nearly vertical and when the lamp had to be brought down in the morning and put back in the afternoon, only one hand was available for a proper hold.

For day-to-day maintenance the whole line was divided into sections of about two miles each. One such section was from the north end of Oxenholme station to Peat Lane signal box, a distance of just under two miles. This was looked after by a foreman ganger, who always wore a bowler hat, and two platelayers. Their hut and headquarters was just south of Birklands Bridge. They always seemed to be busy on the track and in the summer they also mowed the grass beside the line and trimmed the hedges.

It was of course the Locomotive Department which employed the greatest number of men. Mr Collins, complete with bowler hat and umbrella, was the shedmaster until 1915 when he was replaced by Mr Bunner, who wore a soft hat and did not have an umbrella. There must have been 25 to 30 drivers and firemen. The foreman fitter was Campbell and he had two or three men working with him, and then there were the men who worked on the coaling plant and ash pits, which must have been really gruelling work.

Finally there was the clerk in the shed office. I knew him quite well but never discovered his name. He used to come up on to the station to meet the 'Road Van'. This was a short train of only two or

A 'Cauliflower' or '18in Goods', one of the class which often worked the 'Road Van". This is No. 34 and the date is probably about 1900 but its immaculate condition is typical of the whole period up to the beginning of the First World War. From a distance, the LNWR coat of arms on the driving splasher was said to look like a cauliflower, which gave the class its nickname.

A view of Oxenholme shed about 1900 with various members of the shed staff posed for the camera. On the right is a '17in Coal Engine' in full lined black livery and in the centre is a 'Jumbo'.

This rather sad view of the shed was taken on 5th June 1965, after closure, but at least it shows the same layout as in LNWR days. Wagons of coal were shunted up the ramp on the left under the water tank and the coal was then shovelled by labourers directly into engines drawn up along the track to the left of the coal stage. Further along the same track was the turntable. It was only large enough for a 'Jumbo' or 'Cauliflower'. Larger engines such as 'Experiments', '19in Goods' or 'B' class 0-8-0 compounds had to turn at Windermere.

F. W. Shuttleworth

three vans, which arrived at a quiet time in the afternoon. It went north one day and came back south the next, and was usually headed by a 'Jumbo' or '18in Goods'. The purpose of the 'Road Van' was to carry stores and other requirements to the stations and engine sheds along the line. When the train brought spare parts for Oxenholme, the clerk would come and check they were what was wanted. Spares from Crewe were often heavy – sometimes there would be a complete brick arch, or rather all the bricks to make one – and so they were loaded from the 'Road Van' on to a platform trolley. Then when an Oxenholme engine returned light down the bank from Grayrigg, they were transferred on to the engine running plate and ferried down to the shed.

About that time, 1914, firemen were paid extra for firing superheated engines and a list of them was pinned up in the shed. When I heard about this, I mentioned it to the clerk and he brought it out from the shed so that I could make a copy; I returned it to him later. I have often thought about this extra payment. Since the superheated engines were more economical, the fireman's work would surely have been less but perhaps this had not then been established in those early days.

Oxenholme Shed in 1911

The allocation of the shed in 1911 consisted of three 'Precursors', four or five '6ft Jumbos', two or three four-cylinder compound coal engines, two '18in Goods' and one '5ft 6in 2-4-2 Tank'. The 'Precursors' were the top-link passenger engines, while the 'Jumbos' handled local passenger work on the main line and down the branch, and also assisted over Shap. As time went on, the '6ft Jumbos' were replaced by '6ft 6in Jumbos'. The compound coal engines were used on long-distance goods turns.

One of the '18in Goods', No. 455, was used for passenger traffic and any other jobs that turned up but the other was invariably sent to shunt the yard at Kendal. After No. 455, the '18in Goods' at Oxenholme were at various times Nos. 1232, 318, 319 and 476. The '5ft 6in 2-4-2 Tank' was used on short-distance passenger work down the branch and on the main line. At first it was No. 2134, which was replaced by No. 466, which was in turn replaced by No. 1386. About 1915-16 it was decided to try a push-and-pull train on the Windermere branch and a two-coach unit duly arrived with '4ft 6in 2-4-2 Tank' No. 523 attached. This engine was replaced by No. 908 in 1917. This arrangement lasted only for a few

A '5ft 6in 2-4-2 Tank', LMS No. 6632. These engines were normally used on local passenger work such as between Windermere and Grange-over-Sands but during the First World War, when there was a severe shortage of power, were even used occasionally on banking.

years until it was discontinued. On occasions when idle the '4ft 6in 2-4-2 Tank' was given a banking job to Grayrigg but the assistance it could give was only minimal and it was seldon used for this purpose

The Line Over Shap

Oxenholme's importance resulted from its situation 40 miles north of Preston and 50 miles south of Carlisle on what was the most spectacular section of the whole of the London & North Western Railway. As the Lancaster & Carlisle Railway, this line was authorised by Act of Parliament in 1844 to be 70 miles in length from a point one mile south of the present Lancaster station, now known as Lancaster Junction, through to Carlisle. The first 20 miles to Oxenholme was opened on 22nd September 1846, along with a two-mile branch to Kendal, and the rest of the line through to Carlisle was completed on 17th December 1846. In view of the mountainous country through which the line was built, it was a wonderful achievement to build it so quickly. Joseph Locke was the engineer and Thomas Brassey, who at one time had a thousand men working for him, was the contractor.

Even in 1911 there were still one or two reminders of the original Lancaster & Carlisle. The first signal box north of Oxenholme was two miles up the bank and was called Peat Lane – presumably named after the road going off to the left. The box was adjacent to the very steep road from Kendal to Sedbergh, which passed under an iron-girder bridge that was put up when the line was built. The two outside girders, one facing up the road and the other down, had the inscription 'Lancaster & Carlisle Railway 1846' cast on the outer sides in raised letters. These girders were made locally. When the bridge was renewed by the LMS, a report in the *Westmorland Gazette* stated: 'They were foundered in the Lound Iron Foundry,

Kendal'. The new bridge was of concrete and the old girders went to a scrap merchant in Workington.

The highest point of the Lancaster & Carlisle line is Shap Summit, which is 986ft above sea level, and to that point from Hest Bank, where the line skirts the sea shore, is 31$\frac{1}{2}$ miles. So in that distance trains have to climb about 980ft. By coincidence it is also 31$\frac{1}{2}$ miles from the top down the other side to Carlisle. When Locke planned his route he chose to take the line up the Kent Valley to the east of Kendal, cross the high ground eastwards to the Lune Valley, go north up the Lune Gorge to Tebay and then make the final climb to the summit.

The really serious climbing actually begins at Milnthorpe, six miles south of Oxenholme. From there the line starts to climb up the high ground to the east of the valley of the River Kent. The climbing continues through Oxenholme after which the line looks down on Kendal, which is really a shortened form of 'Kent Dale'. It passes through Peat Lane and comes to Hay Fell where it begins to turn to the right in a very deep rock cutting. At this point it has now left the eastern side of Kent Dale and is on the lower shoulders of Benson Knot, which is over 1000ft high and is the highest point on the ridge. The line then comes round to Lambrigg Crossing after passing over Docker Viaduct, which is quite high, with the river in a ravine beneath. Like all the viaducts and bridges on the line, Docker Viaduct was built of local limestone. Then the line comes to Mosedale Hall and Grayrigg, which is seven miles from Oxenholme. By this point it has climbed out of the Kent Valley.

The line between Oxenholme No. 3 and Grayrigg was divided into five block sections by the boxes at Peat Lane, Hay Fell, Lambrigg Crossing and Mosedale Hall. Each successive block section was shorter than the previous one so as to make it easier to keep the traffic moving as the gradient pulled the speed down.

A 'Superheater Goods Class G1' (to give the official name of the class), LMS No. 9023, trundles down the hill into Oxenholme with an up goods. No. 3 signal box is on the right and the Windermere branch is on the left.

H. Gordon Tidey

'19in Goods' 4-6-0 No. 1512 leaving Oxenholme with a down goods.

H. Gordon Tidey

Grayrigg station about 1900, looking east from the west end of the up platform.

Bernard Matthews collection

A '17in Coal Engine' just north of Hay Fell box where the line comes out of a cutting into the open and turns right towards Grayrigg. The engine is fully lined and is well cleaned and polished. It will take its train of empty coke wagons, which have come from Ulverston, as far as Tebay, where they will be taken on by a North Eastern Railway engine via Stainmore to destinations in the Darlington area. The date is sometime in the early 1900s.

The scene at Grayrigg box about 1900, as a down passenger train passes the signal box. It seems likely that the 'Small Jumbo' on the right, No. 469 *St. George,* has piloted the train from Oxenholme to Grayrigg and has just hooked off, leaving the train engine, another 'Small Jumbo' to proceed unaided as far as Tebay.

Low Gill station looking north sometime in the early 1900s. The main lines are on the left, curving into the Lune Gorge, with a cant of 11in. On the right is the line to Ingleton; a '17in Coal Engine' seems to be marshalling its train before proceeding along the branch.

Bernard Matthews collection

Grayrigg station is in a dip and the line now goes through this dip and falls for nearly two miles to Low Gill, where there is a very sharp left-hand curve which takes it into the Lune Gorge, with the Yorkshire mountains on the right-hand side and the Westmorland mountains on the left. The curve at Low Gill was the sharpest on the whole of the LNWR main line. To ensure a train could traverse it safely at a speed of 55 miles an hour, the outside rail at the centre of the curve was canted eleven inches higher than the inside rail. It must surely have been a work of art to build such a curve to rise gradually to its maximum at its mid point and then fade it out again.

This information about Low Gill curve came from a former Permanent Way Inspector, who before he retired was responsible for the maintenance of the line from Preston to Carlisle. I only met him once. He was talking to Jack Speed on the up platform at Oxenholme one day and I joined them. After Jack had left, I had a most interesting conversation with him. Among other things he told me that whenever he wanted to check the line he always rode on the footplate of a 'Claughton'. These engines were very smooth-riding and so if they rolled or rocked, the reason was that the track at that particular point was at fault and needed attention.

Once through Low Gill there are four miles of easy track to Tebay. At about the mid point was Dillicar signal box – it was located just below Dillicar Fell, which gave it its name – and then just before Tebay were Dillicar troughs, which were the last set of water troughs before Carlisle. The river, road and

'Prince of Wales' No. 2249 *Thomas Campbell* taking water from Dillicar troughs with an up express about 1914. *H. Gordon Tidey*

An up goods south of Tebay hauled by 'Prince of Wales' LMS No. 25641 *Czar of Russia*. It is about to pass under the bridge carrying the Kendal to Tebay road over to the east side of the line. On the left is the down slow line used at this point by goods trains which were to be overtaken at Tebay while taking a banker.

railway all traverse this section through the Lune Gorge together. The scenery is the finest between London and Carlisle. It is a magnificent sight in summer sunshine and perhaps even more so in winter snow. The speed of express trains rose rapidly over this stretch to seventy miles an hour or more when passing through Tebay. This enabled them to get a good run at the final four-mile climb on a gradient of 1 in 75 to Shap Summit.

In the days of the 'Precursors' and 'Experiments' Oxenholme 'Jumbos' used to work through to Carlisle assisting and then assist an up train back as far as Oxenholme. Carlisle 'Jumbos' used to do the same thing from the Carlisle end. That all stopped when the superheated engines took over. They did not usually need assistance anyway but when an assisting engine was needed, it came off at Shap Summit and returned light to Oxenholme. The reason

for this presumably was that assisting engines were only needed occasionally, whereas previously they could be rostered as all trains took them.

Oxenholme men said that when assisting passenger trains from a standing start at Oxenholme they reckoned to be at Shap Summit, 18½ miles away, in 26 minutes. They reckoned about 11 minutes for the 7 miles up to Grayrigg with both engines slogging hard up the bank all the time, then a couple of minutes through the dip to Low Gill, 5 minutes over the fast stretch to Tebay and then 8 minutes up to the top of Shap. The train would stop at the summit and the assisting engine would hook off and run back light down to Oxenholme. From Shap Summit of course the work of the fireman of the main-line train was virtually finished as it was downhill all the way to Carlisle. He would just have to make sure that the fire was burning down nicely and evenly, because

Tebay station looking north from the south end of the down platform.

Bernard Matthews collection

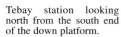

19

One of Mr Whale's 'Experiment' class 4-6-0s, No. 667 *Mazeppa,* just north of Tebay attacking the climb to Shap unaided with a very sizeable down express.

One of the first batch of 'Prince of Wales' 4-6-0s, No. 1691 *Pathfinder,* climbing Shap unaided with a 12-coach down express. The location is Shap Wells and the date about 1920.

'Prince of Wales' No. 86 *Mark Twain* with an up goods from Kingmoor yard at Etterby Junction about 1920.

An up express leaving Carlisle behind 4-6-2 'Superheater Tank' No. 1692 and a 'Prince of Wales' early in LMS days. The 4-6-2 tank will come off at either Tebay or Oxenholme.

nobody would thank him if he went on the shed with a big fire at Carlisle, especially if the engine was to be turned and the fire cleaned for a quick return to the south.

Goods trains which needed assistance were banked from Oxenholme only as far as Grayrigg and the banker returned light to Oxenholme from there. The train engine then proceeded on its own to Tebay and took another banker from there to Shap. At one time passenger trains were banked in the rear from Oxenholme; but after some of the carriages of one became buffer-locked on the sharp curve at Hay Fell one day, it was laid down that they were to be assisted in front right through to Shap Summit.

The climb up to Shap could be a very thrilling ride, especially with a heavy train and two engines going hard on a dark winter's night. It was something all the men looked forward to, because it came as a thrilling interlude in what they were doing at the time. Assisting to Shap was one of the duties of the extra-link men. There were six sets of men in this link, and they got all the extra jobs that came along. They drove anything and went anywhere, and often did not know where they were going next. So they got wonderful experience of different kinds of traffic

and of working on different parts of the line. Unfortunately, I never had a ride to Shap on an engine, or even to Grayrigg. Jack Armer once said he would take me to Grayrigg on a banker but I was never on the platform when he was on that duty.

The proper procedure for a driver of a passenger train to obtain an assisting engine from Oxenholme was by means of the telegraph. If a driver taking a train over at Crewe, for example, knew by the load that he would need assistance, he would ask the foreman on the platform to wire to Oxenholme 'XJA', which was the telegraphic code for 'Provide Assisting Engine'. The foreman would add the time the train left, 5.19pm for the 'Corridor', and the weight of the train, say, 430 tons. When he arrived at Oxenholme – the 'Corridor' was due to pass at 7.08pm – he would stop his train with the engine alongside the shed by No. 2 box and the assistant engine, which would be waiting for him, would back down on to the front. Even before the First World War there were always some trains that were very heavy and needed assistance up to Shap Summit, and Oxenholme used to use 'Jumbos' both for hooking on and banking. During the war, however, the number requiring assistance increased greatly.

21

Scene at Carlisle Citadel station shortly after the Grouping. A '6ft 6in Jumbo' in LMS livery, No. 5012 *John Ramsbottom,* and a Lancashire & Yorkshire Railway four-cylinder 4-6-0, still carrying its L&Y number 1670, await the arrival of an express from the north which they will take over for the southbound run over Shap.

Sometimes, of course, a driver would leave Crewe or Preston thinking he could climb Shap unassisted but would decide en route that he needed an assisting engine. Perhaps his engine was not steaming well or some defect had developed. Whatever the reason, there were two things he could do apart from making a special stop somewhere to use the telegraph. He could attract the attention of a signalman by crowing on the whistle and indicate to him by hooking his fingers together that he wanted an engine to hook on; the signalman would then telephone Oxenholme. Alternatively, he could just stop by the shed at Oxenholme as if to say, 'Here I am? What can you do about it?'

One hot summer's day in 1914 I was sitting on the coping of the overbridge by No. 2 box, when that happened. The 10am from Euston arrived and stopped by the shed. Normally it ran in two parts, the Glasgow portion passing Oxenholme at 2.47pm and the Edinburgh portion at 2.53pm, but for some reason that day the two were combined into one big train. In the summer sunshine it looked perfect, the chocolate and cream carriages and a 'Prince of Wales' new off the works in January, No. 1400 *Felicia Hemans,* all polished up to the nines. He had stopped for assistance without having wired.

The signalman came to his window and the driver signalled to him that he wanted an assistant engine by hooking his fingers together. The signalman phoned to the shed and everybody sat and waited. Eventually Mr Collins, the shedmaster, came out round the end of the shed, walked up towards the box and called up to the signalman, 'I haven't any engines here. Are any of my engines coming down the bank?'

The signalman said, 'No, there are none of yours coming down but there is one coming down. He's going further south. I don't know where to'.

At this, Mr Collins replied, 'Stop him.' He then walked up underneath the bridge and on to the end of the down platform where he stopped and waited opposite where the engine would stop. The signalman had put the signal back to danger and when the engine came into sight, I saw it was a '6ft 6in Jumbo', the same type that Oxenholme would have used for assisting anyway. When it came to a stand, I could see that Mr Collins was telling the driver he was going to have to cross over and help the 'Corridor' up to Shap Summit before continuing his journey south. There seemed to be a bit of discussion going on but nobody argued with Mr Collins for long and in the end he turned to face the signalbox and lifted his crossed arms to indicate the engine was to cross over. So the points were set and the engine crossed over and started to back down on to the front of the 'Corridor'.

It was No. 2002 *Madge.* What a contrast! The 'Jumbo' was filthy. It looked as if it had not been cleaned for months. I do not know why not. In addition, of course, it had no steam up as it had been running light down Shap. The fireman was busy firing up, and black smoke was coming out of the chimney, in an effort to raise some steam to get them up to Shap. When they started away, the driver of the 'Jumbo' took his brakes off but did no more. The 'Prince of Wales' lifted the whole train and the 'Jumbo' under the bridge, right through the station and up to the advance starting signal before the 'Jumbo' began to open up.

'Experiment' No. 565 *City of Carlisle* standing in Oxenholme station sometime in 1915. Driver Jack Speed, one of Oxenholme's top-link drivers, and his fireman are looking out at the photographer.   *W. L. Harris*

Driver Jack Speed standing beside his engine, *City of Carlisle*, on the same occasion. His fireman is on his left and is either his own son or Richard Haythornthwaite.   *W. L. Harris*

On another occasion in the evening, instead of the usual 'Jumbo', I saw a 'Claughton', No. 650 *Lord Rathmore*, banking a goods train towards Grayrigg. The driver was Jack Armer and he told me later that it had been taken off one of the night sleepers with a hot bearing. The bearing had been repaired at Oxenholme shed and they were running it in again on banking.

The Top Link

The top passenger link at Oxenholme had three sets of men, all of whom had 'Precursors'. One of them was Jack Speed, whom with his engine No. 374 *Empress* I had met on my first visit to the station. The other two were Dick Laycock, whose engine was No. 1364 *Clyde*, and Jack Thornborough, whose engine was No. 2553 *Teutonic*, which after the war broke out was first renamed *The Tsar* and then *Moonstone*.

Jack Speed liked to tell the story of how he once came down from Shap Summit to Tebay, a distance of five miles, in four minutes with a train of old six-wheelers which shook from side to side. When he stopped at Tebay, an elderly clergyman came along the platform waving his umbrella at him. He said he was going to report him and he did. Jack was called to the District Superintendent's office at Lancaster and lost a day's pay.

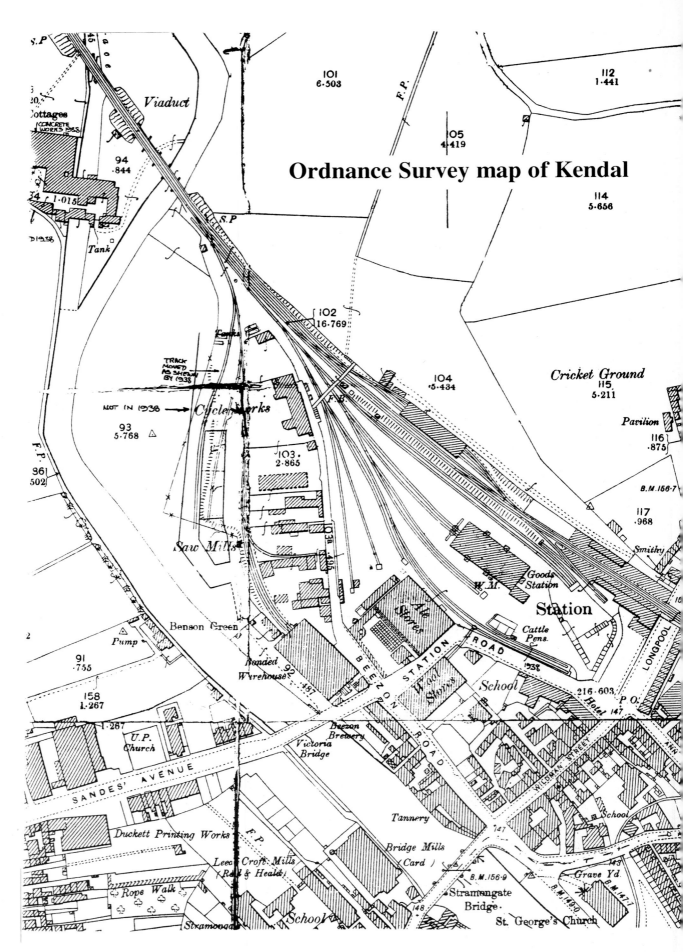

Ordnance Survey map of Kendal

24

East Bank

84
1·495

85 ·481

86
1·588

MINT STREET

87
3·417

153

Pump

89
1·196

88
·953

B.S

F.W.

Corn Mill

121
1·457

F.W.

122
1·800

126
2·112

90
2·751

134
3·249

133
1·806

131
·265

91 ·337

F.W.

S t o c k

B e c k

127
7·027

Auction Mart

123
1·322

125
10·010

128
3·504

N O R T H

Inn

119
·677

124
3·833

153
3·267

118
·502

S.P

157
1·589

P

Allotment
Gardens

1·589

156
3·848

155
4·452

3·848

4·952

2·10

3·267 2·253

219
1·066

Eller Lea J. Morris 14·10·1924.

365 sq yds sold to Fk. Griffiths.
Agt. dated 17th Sept. 1938.

220
·595

154
2·710

Lodge

CEMETERY

166

Brantholme

Mortuary
Chapel

218
·738

221
2·007

Heathfield

242
·448

Main-line passenger engines used to go into the works for general overhaul about every fourteen months. When a driver lost his engine in this way, he very rarely got it back again. Instead it was replaced by another one which had just been overhauled. So over the period from 1911 Jack Speed had a number of engines. After the 'Precursor' *Empress* went to Crewe, he had four 'Experiments' in turn: 1412 *Bedfordshire*, 1621 *Denbighshire*, 565 *City of Carlisle* and 1477 *Hugh Myddleton*.

Jack Speed's fireman's name was Anthony Haythornthwaite though he was commonly called 'Tant'. He used to keep a list of all the named engines as he saw them. When an engine was scrapped, he put an 'X' beside it and for many years I did the same. He lent me his list and I made my first proper lists from it.

I liked Dick Laycock. He was a big man, confident and quiet. His son, who was older than I was, also went to the Grammar School in Kendal. Dick told me he had tried to get his son into the drawing office at Crewe but without success. He succeeded, however, in getting him into the North Eastern Railway drawing office in Darlington and he told me that he and his wife would move there when he finished working.

He retired on Friday 3rd July 1914. I knew he would be working the 6.45pm from Windermere to Preston, so I was on the up platform at Oxenholme just after 7pm to see him. When the train came in, he got down from his engine and we had a few words till the guard waved him away. He then shook hands with me and climbed back on to his engine, and before I realised it he was gone. I never saw him again.

I was only a boy of fourteen at the time and I thought it was wonderful that a top-link driver should step down on to the platform to say goodbye to me. He was a great 'Precursor' man and his engines were: Nos. 1364 *Clyde*, 1387 *Lang Meg* and 2181 *Eleanor*. He was replaced in the top link by Walter Phyzackerley whose engine was 'Experiment' No. 1709 *Princess May*. He was a great big tall chap. I quite liked him and got on well with him too.

There were three top-link turns worked by the passenger drivers at Oxenholme. The drivers all kept their own engines of course and they worked round the three trips in turn, so that they had each one every third week. Two were long turns, one to Manchester and the other to Crewe, which were twelve-hour days, and the third was a short turn to Preston in the afternoon.

The first turn, to Manchester, was the 8.30am 'Manchester Club Train' from Windermere, which left Kendal at 8.42am. The engine for this train was worked into Windermere by extra-link men and they then worked the 'Manchester Club Train' as far as Kendal. The top-link driver and his fireman travelled down to Kendal on the light engine that was going to shunt Kendal yard all day. At that time this engine was '18in Goods' No. 1232. On arriving in Kendal they put the engine in the carriage dock, screwed the brake on hard, left it and crossed over to the other platform to wait for the 8.30am from Windermere. When the 'Club Train' arrived, the extra-link men stepped off and the top-link men took over. This train called at Lancaster, Preston and Wigan and arrived in Manchester (Exchange) at 10.30am. They then hooked off, turned the engine and worked a 40-minute express from Manchester (Exchange) to Liverpool (Lime Street). When they got to the shed at Edge Hill, they booked off for their lunch break. Sometime in the afternoon they worked another 40-minute express back to Manchester. On arrival, the engine was turned again for the trip back to Windermere on the 4.15pm 'Club Train' from Exchange. At Oxenholme they were relieved by extra men who took the train on to Windermere, disposed of the stock and brought the engine back light to Oxenholme.

The 'Club Train' comprised six eight-wheeled bogie carriages with an eight-wheeled open saloon for the members of the club inserted in the middle and weighed about 210 tons. On Saturdays the saloon was removed from the train and it then weighed only about 180 tons. The saloon was open and was furnished with armchairs and writing tables; it had its own lavatory compartment complete with wash-basin. The other carriages were non-corridor and had both first and third class compartments; each compartment had access to a lavatory through a door in the middle of one of the seats. The two end carriages were half guard's van.

The second long trip was the 11.25am from Windermere through to Crewe. Once again the engine was worked into Windermere by extra men who then brought the train as far as Oxenholme where the top-link driver and fireman were waiting for it at 11.57am. The extra men stepped down and the top-link men took over and went through to Crewe. They returned in the afternoon with the 5.50pm from Crewe to Windermere. On arrival at Oxenholme, they were relieved by extra men who took the train on to Windermere, disposed of the stock and brought the engine back light to Oxenholme.

The third trip was what they called the 'short' trip. They booked on at 3pm and came off the shed at 3.45pm with their engine facing north, ran through the station, crossed over on to the up line and then went forward on to the short line alongside No. 3 signal box to await the arrival of the stopping train from Carlisle which was due at 4.17pm and terminated there. In 1911 it was often brought in by a Carlisle 'Experiment', such as No. 2076 *Pheasant* or 2116 *Greystoke*. When that train arrived, they backed down on to the back of it and the engine that had

A 'Cauliflower' coming off the Windermere branch and crossing over into platform 1 at Oxenholme with the 4.25pm from Windermere, which served all stations to Lancaster and Preston. For a long time it was worked by Driver Bill Duckett with '18in Goods' No. 455. From Oxenholme the train was taken forward by the engine which had arrived at 4.17pm on a stopping train from Carlisle and had since been waiting in the up loop.

W. L. Harris

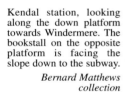

Kendal station, looking along the down platform towards Windermere. The bookstall on the opposite platform is facing the slope down to the subway.

Bernard Matthews collection

brought it in was uncoupled and went forward into the up loop beyond No. 2 box to await the 4.25pm train from Windermere, which it worked forward to Preston. In 1911 the 4.25pm from Windermere was invariably worked into Oxenholme by '18in Goods' No. 455 in charge of Bill Duckett. On arrival the engine was detached and went to the shed.

Then the 'Aberdeen' arrived, which was the 10.30am general purpose train from Euston, due at 4.32pm. This train was divided at Oxenholme and the first portion departed up the 'high line' to Carlisle (the 'low line', as we called it, was the one to Kendal). The Oxenholme driver then crossed over with the empty stock off the 4.17pm arrival from Carlisle and backed down on to the carriages left

behind by the 'Aberdeen' in the station. After coupling up, they took the whole train through to Windermere, where the engine was detached and turned, and then worked the 6.45pm from Windermere to Preston. They returned from Preston with the last train into Kendal, where it arrived at 10.15pm. The men disposed of the carriages at Kendal and returned light engine to Oxenholme.

One day Walter Phyzackerley with No. 1709 *Princess May* was on this turn. He had backed down on to the 4.17pm arrival from Carlisle and was standing in the platform on the up main line. I was standing on the platform alongside his engine when all of a sudden the signalman pulled all the signals off as if there was an up express coming through. I

27

One of the 'Claughtons', No. 1567 *Charles J. Cropper*, was named after a member of the Cropper family; their family home was at Tolson Hall and they owned paper mills at Burneside and Bowston. The engine is seen here at Camden about 1920.

thought 'That's a bit strange' but anyway I told Walter and he looked through his spectacle glass and then whistled as hard as he could. This brought the signalman to his window and he called down 'Testing', so we said 'OK'. He was testing the signals but if he had been testing us we would have passed too.

Sometime about 1915-16 Oxenholme men lost the working of the 'Club Train' to Preston men. They worked the 3.33am mail train from Preston, arriving at Windermere at about 5.45am, and returned with the 8.30am 'Club Train' through to Manchester (Exchange), arriving at 10.30am. This meant that Oxenholme then had only two top-link jobs, the two top-link drivers being Jack Speed and Walter Phyzackerley.

Traffic on the Windermere branch

In those days Kendal was a thriving market town with various industries, including a woollen mill, a boot and shoe factory ('K Shoes'), a leather tannery and drysalters, and several other smaller businesses. A few miles away at Mealbank there was another woollen mill and at Burneside there were two paper mills belonging to the Cropper family. 'Claughton' No. 1567 *Charles J. Cropper* was named after a leading member of this family, incidentally, and when new in September 1914 was allocated to Carlisle. One evening soon afterwards it replaced the engine of the 'Club Train' on arrival at Oxenholme from Manchester and worked it down the branch to Windermere, just to show the people of Burneside that the local family had been recognised by the railway company. In addition to the traffic generated by these industries, the products and requirements of the farming community produced quite a lot of traffic also, as the line passed through good agricultural land.

The traffic on the branch was therefore quite sizeable. It was worked by morning and afternoon branch goods trains and by two long-distance turns, the Liverpool goods and the Wigan goods, which ran through to and from Windermere. The inward Liverpool goods was worked by Edge Hill men, who presumably booked off at Oxenholme and returned to Edge Hill in the evening. Oxenholme men relieved them and worked the train down the branch. It was a tedious job, dropping wagons off at every yard and siding to Windermere. In the summer of 1914, their engines were new 'Superheater Goods' Nos. 2379, 48, 62 and 72. They were fully painted and lined and were a wonderful sight.

The Wigan goods was worked by Oxenholme men. The outward working departed late in the evening and the return was the following day, so that the men must have lodged at Wigan. For this trip Oxenholme used four-cylinder compound goods engines Nos 134, 1240, 2169 and 2570. Nos. 134 and 1240 were as originally built (class 'B') but No. 2169 was class 'E' (with pony truck added at the front end) and No. 2570 was class 'F' (with pony truck and large boiler). No. 134 was the engine which blew up at Buxton in 1921 due to its safety valves being incorrectly repaired by an outside contractor. In 1918-19 the four-cylinder compound goods engines at Oxenholme were replaced by 'Superheater Goods Class G1'.

After the Grouping Oxenholme men worked all the goods traffic to and from both Liverpool and Wigan, as well as the morning and afternoon goods to Windermere and back to Oxenholme. They then had six 'Superheater Goods Class G1', LMS Nos. 9325-30, which had previously been LNWR Nos 1261, 1306, 1487, 1793, 2287 and 279.

Burneside station with its staggered platforms about 1900. There was no signal box; the porter operated the levers in the frame on the right as required. Normally the 'Club Train' to Manchester did not stop here but on Tuesdays a special stop was made to pick up a representative from the nearby paper-manufacturing firm of Cropper's, who travelled to Manchester on business.

Bernard Matthews collection

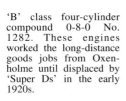

Another view of Burneside, with a Webb 2-4-2 tank about to leave on a train to Kendal and Oxenholme. The down platform is out of the picture to the right.

Bernard Matthews collection

'B' class four-cylinder compound 0-8-0 No. 1282. These engines worked the long-distance goods jobs from Oxenholme until displaced by 'Super Ds' in the early 1920s.

There were two 2-8-0 variants of the 'B' class, the 'E' class with small boiler and the 'F' class with large. This is 'E' class LMS No. 9603, formerly LNWR No. 2558.

W. H. Whitworth

Windermere station from the approach road about 1910.

Bernard Matthews collection

View of Windermere shed in the late 1920s with '19in Goods' class 4-6-0, LMS No. 8848, posed on the turntable (for which it is too long!). In the left background is a wagon of the Ullswater Gunpowder Co. Ltd.

Bernard Matthews collection

30

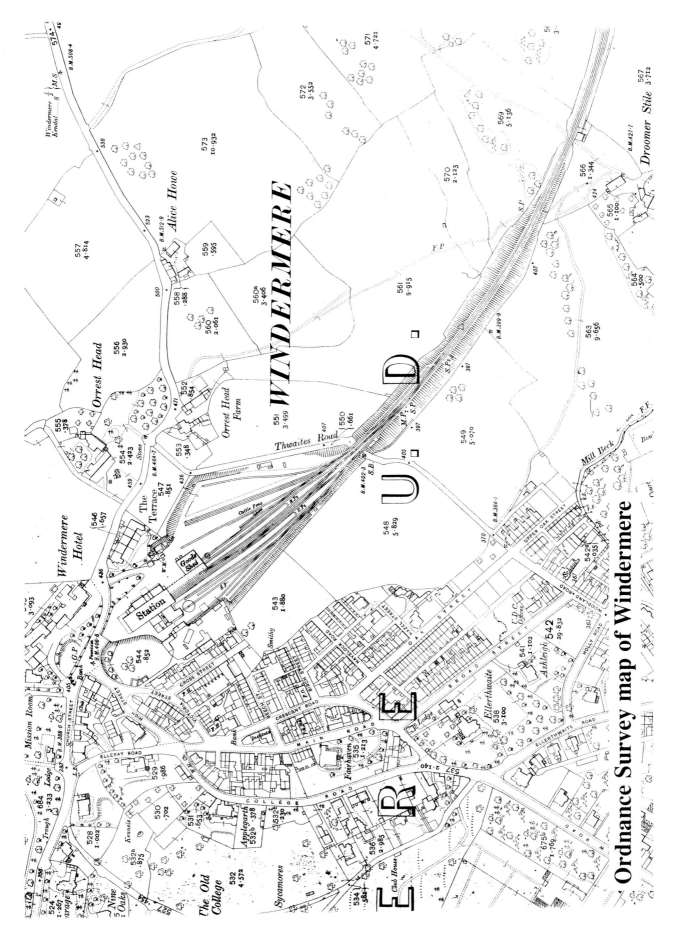

Ordnance Survey map of Windermere

31

'Superheater Tank' No. 1692 climbing away from Oxenholme with the 'market train' returning from Kendal to Ingleton. This operated on Saturdays only to bring passengers from Ingleton and stations on the main line to the market at Kendal. It was worked by a Tebay engine, which first ran light to Ingleton, where the stock was stored overnight, worked to Low Gill, ran round and then down to Oxenholme, ran round again and then took the branch to Kendal. On the return journey of course it ran round twice again before reaching Ingleton.

H. Gordon Tidey

A Liverpool and Manchester to Glasgow and Edinburgh express passing Oxenholme. This train was combined at Preston and left there at 1.38pm, passing Oxenholme at 2.22pm. By the time the picture was taken it was usually worked by a superheater engine but that day there was presumably not one available. The 'Experiment' stopped for assistance on the other side of the bridge and Oxenholme 'Big Jumbo' No. 1675 *Vimiera* was attached. In the picture the train is just restarting. The bridge carries the Kendal to New Hutton road over the line and the high signal box is No. 2, which controlled the north end of the yard and the entrance to the station. The locomotive shed is immediately behind it.

W. L. Harris

One of the four Furness Railway 4-4-2 tanks Nos. 39-42, which were built by Kitson, arriving at Oxenholme with a stopping passenger train from Grange-over-Sands. The working of these trains was shared by the Furness and LNWR. Before the 4-4-2 tanks appeared, the FR often used 2-4-2 tanks Nos. 72 and 74.

W. L. Harris

Furness Railway 0-6-0 No. 9 near Grange-over-Sands with a train of empty mineral wagons from Ulverston to the North Eastern Railway via Tebay. These trains were referred to as 'birdcage specials', because of the open rails on the top of the wagons; the telegraph code for empty wagon trains such as these was OBY.

On Saturdays there were two local passenger trains which were run specially for the market at Kendal, arriving in the morning and returning in the afternoon. One came from Lancaster and was always worked by '5ft 6in 2-4-2 Tank' No. 649. The other came from Ingleton and was always headed by No. 546 of the same class from Tebay shed. The engine had to run round its train twice in each direction, at Low Gill and at Oxenholme.

Other stopping trains were operated by the Furness Railway from Grange to Kendal twice a day. The first trip was early in the morning bringing people from Grange to Kendal and boys and girls to school. Its route was over the viaduct at Arnside to Hincaster Junction, then over the London & North Western Railway to Oxenholme and down to Kendal. It then returned to Grange and came back again to Kendal at about 5pm, before going back once again to Grange. In the early days it was worked by a Furness Railway 2-4-2 tank but later a 4-4-2 tank took over.

After the Grouping, Oxenholme men from the 'Old Man's Link' worked a local passenger turn at 8.40am

from Windermere to Grange-over-Sands, via Hincaster Junction and Arnside, and returned later, and there must have been a similar working in the late afternoon. In fact, that was about as far as the 'Old Man's Link' went, down the branch to Windermere and to Grange-over-Sands; they were employed on any local work that cropped up.

Before the war the Furness Railway had a share in the extensive traffic in coke from the Darlington area to the ironworks at Ulverston. The North Eastern brought it to Tebay and from there the traffic was shared equally and worked jointly by the London & North Western and Furness Railways. Furness engines worked through to Tebay, mostly six-coupled goods, and the LNWR engines worked right through to Ulverston; they were usually '18in Goods', commonly known as 'Cauliflowers', of which there were quite a number stationed at Tebay. Because the loaded wagons were worked downhill and the empty wagons uphill, there was no need for these trains to be banked to Grayrigg.

33

No. 2 Signal Box

After a while I got to know one of the signalmen in No. 2 box. He used to invite me up into his box in the evenings and we became very friendly. I enjoyed my time with him as it was very interesting in the box. He used to let me ring the bells and pull the signals, while he worked the points and kept the book.

One summer evening we were sitting in the signal box when we had word from the telegraph office on the station that the up 'Postal' which was due to pass at 9.51pm was 10 minutes late from Carlisle. It was a lovely evening, very quiet, and we had the windows open. If the 'Postal' had been on time, we would have expected a ring on the bell at about 9.45pm. That would be when the train was approaching Grayrigg. We knew this because Low Gill did not offer a train forward until he got 'entering section' from the previous box, Dillicar. This was because Low Gill was one of those boxes on the line that were designated as 'holding points'; they would not offer a train on any further until they got 'entering section' from the previous box. The point of this was that if every box offered a train on as soon as they got it, trains would be offered to Crewe and London before they had got to Preston. So there had to be 'holding points' at certain places. Low Gill was one and the next going south was Milnthorpe. Going north from Low Gill the next was Shap Summit.

Anyway, just after 9.40pm the bell rang. I looked at the signalman and he looked at me. Then I said, 'It can't be anything else but the "Postal",' and the signalman agreed. So I rang 1-2-3-4 to acknowledge, offered it on to No. 1 box and pulled the signals off. Sure enough it was the 'Postal'. It came through dead on time at 9.51pm with two engines on. They had covered the 50 miles from Carlisle in 50 minutes instead of the scheduled 60 minutes and despite having to climb Shap they had made up 10 minutes.

Of course, the postal people inside the train would be sorting all the time and they did not really like the drivers to make up time because then they had less time to sort. On leaving Carlisle, the 'Postal' picked up without stopping at Penrith and at Oxenholme and was first stop Carnforth where it was due to stop from 10.05 to 10.15pm. They stopped there because there was always a lot of mail to be loaded from the Furness, places like Barrow and Whitehaven, and other places round the coast, and from the Midland lines across to Keighley and Skipton.

Picking Up The Mails

My father used to hold a Sunday afternoon class for young men that was absolutely non-denominational. They would come along at 2 o'clock, and most of the time would be spent singing hymns. Then there would be a little address, which they could either accept or think about as they pleased, and then they used to leave at about 2.50pm. If anyone missed a meeting, my father made a point of seeing him during the week and finding out if he was ill or had any problems.

The class attracted men from all walks of life and thanks to this personal touch it grew more and more popular. Eventually it became too big for my father to run single-handed and so a committee was formed to help him. The meetings were held in Gillingate Mission Hall. There were about 500 names on the books and the average attendance was 350. It was wonderful to hear so many men singing, and the wives and girl-friends who used to come to meet them after the class used to arrive early so they could just stand and listen. The organisation became so successful that one evening in the autumn they used to have a supper and concert in a hall in the town for members only. There was plenty of talent among the men who attended. The supper would be served at 7pm and then the concert would follow.

The food for the supper was excellent. It was obtained from the Army & Navy Stores in London and was delivered by overnight passenger train arriving in Kendal on the morning mail at about 5am. This ensured that everything was fresh. The supper and concert was for members only and the only women present were the wives of the men on the committee who set out the tables and organised the food. There was no cooking to be done, just tea and coffee to be made. On the Sunday after the supper and concert there was always a big influx of new members to the class. They had delayed joining until after the supper and were to be respected for that.

Among the men who attended the class was a postman from Kendal called Tom Ewan. One Sunday he asked me if I would like to go up with him to Oxenholme as he was going to take the mails to be picked up without the train stopping and to bring back those that were dropped. I accepted his invitation eagerly and he told me to be at the bottom of Gillingate at half past eight that evening.

I was there before half past eight, of course, and he arrived on time with a pony and trap. It was a two-wheeled trap with room for the two of us in front and for the mails in the back. So off we went, through the town, down through Kirkland, over Nether Bridge, along the Lound and up the Oxenholme Road. Just before we got to the station we turned in a gate on the left where there was a farm and we stopped there. We took the pony out of the trap and put him in the stable. Then we got the mailbags out of the back of the trap and carried them up to an under-bridge over which the main Carlisle line ran. We climbed over the fence and went up a well-worn footpath to the lineside. Then we walked up alongside the line till we came to a wooden level crossing, which was the point where the mails were picked up and dropped on both sides of the line. The actual fitting which supported the bags for down trains was to the north of this crossing and that for up trains was to the south of it on the opposite side, to which we now crossed.

On the up side there was a little wooden hut which was connected by telephone to No. 3 signal box. As soon as Tom had opened the door, he phoned the box to say he had arrived and the signalman replied that he would inform him when the train was on its way. The first train we had mails for was the up 'Limited Postal', which was due to pass Oxenholme at 9.16pm. It was named the 'Limited' because the accommodation for passengers was limited. Two postal vans always came immediately after the engine. They were put there so that all the exchanging of mails would be completed before the other coaches passed and so there would be no danger of passengers putting their heads out and getting injured. The second train was the up 'Postal' which was due to pass at 9.51pm. It consisted entirely of postal vans, 10-12 carriages in all.

The first thing we did was to sort out the mails into two piles, one pile for the 9.16pm and the other for the 9.51pm. Then Tom took two big leather pouches from the store he had in the shed. We put the bags of mail for the 9.16pm into the middle of one of them and Tom tied it up in a special way. We then took it out and hung it up on the post beside the line and opened the net which was on the ground beside the line.

We then waited for the signalman at No. 3 box to tell us that the train was coming. It was not long before he said that the next train would be the up 'Limited Postal', the 9.16pm, so Tom then turned the arm of the post which was holding the pouch so that it was at right angles to the train. We stood and waited by the open door of the shed. Tom had a hand lamp which he shone on to the net and on to the pouch hanging up. As the train went by, there was a sort of bang. Our pouch disappeared into the train and another pouch came off the train and was caught by the top frame of the net. There it was lying on the ground in the net beside the line. The operation was then repeated with the 9.51pm 'Postal'.

After that we packed up and made for home carrying the bags of mail for Kendal. As we set off, I started to cross the level crossing to the path on the far side, the same way that we had come, but Tom said it was best to go down the other side. He explained that one night when he had returned later for the down 'Postal', there was a note in the pouch saying that the up 'Postal' had not picked anything up. So he had searched down the lineside and found the pouch lying there. Something must have made it miss the net on the train. Perhaps a poker or fire-iron on the engine tender had knocked it off. So now he always went that way to make sure nothing had been dropped. Then we carried the bags down to the farm, got the pony and trap hitched up again and came back down to Kendal. We got there about 10.30pm, so had been away for about two hours. Tom of course would go up again at about 2am for the down 'Postal' which was due at 2.14am.

The up and down 'Postals' were purposely timed to be at Crewe at the same time, so that sorters could change over and work back home. At one time there were 147 places in the country where the mails were picked up and dropped without the trains stopping. Now of course they have all been removed. The last to be dismantled was at Penrith.

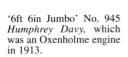

'6ft 6in Jumbo' No. 945 *Humphrey Davy,* which was an Oxenholme engine in 1913.

Roger Carpenter collection

The First World War

The effect of the outbreak of war in 1914 was considerable. Passenger traffic began to be curtailed almost immediately, by combining trains and taking trains off, so as to make engines and men available for goods traffic and special war traffic which increased beyond belief. It put a great strain on the Locomotive Department to keep it all moving and it really brought home to everybody what a big job was being done by the Locomotive Department at Oxenholme. Before the war, for example, there was not a great deal of banking done at all. It was only after war broke out that banking became common.

During the war the down 2pm 'Corridor' from Euston was a very heavy train and often had two engines on all the way from Crewe. One day in July 1917 instead of running through it stopped at Oxenholme with the train engine in trouble. The engines were 'Jumbo' No. 2185 *Alma* and 'Claughton' No. 163 *Holland Hibbert* and Crewe men were in charge as usual. The load was at least 450 tons gross. For some reason the 'Claughton' had failed and had to be removed. It was replaced by Oxenholme 'Jumbo' No. 2186 *Lowther* and Oxenholme men then took the 'Claughton' on to the shed. So that day the 'Corridor' went over Shap hauled by two of Mr Webb's 'Jumbos'. What is more, by coincidence, they were numbered consecutively. Even though a banker was probably taken from Tebay to the Summit, these two little engines put up a great performance with this train.

The down 2pm 'Corridor' was due to pass Oxenholme at 7.08pm and was followed by what we called the 'Second Corridor', which was made up of portions from Manchester and Liverpool. They were combined at Preston, left there at 6.40pm, stopped at Oxenholme from 7.32 to 7.34pm, and called at Penrith before reaching Carlisle. As the war went on, these two trains were combined into one, which ran in the timings of the second. Its weight was consistently between 390 and 420 tons and it normally had two engines on, a Crewe 'Claughton' piloted by a 'Jumbo'. If ever the 'Claughton' brought the train into Oxenholme by itself, it always took an Oxenholme engine to assist it to Shap Summit. The maximum load I saw brought into Oxenholme by a 'Claughton' on this train was 480 tons.

Troop trains and ambulance trains were quite common, of course, and for some reason they always seemed to go through Oxenholme without stopping for an assisting engine. Presumably they were never loaded heavily enough to require one. Ambulance trains seemed to be invariably hauled by a 'George the Fifth' or a 'Rebuilt Precursor'. A lot of them conveyed injured troops to and from country houses in Scotland, which had been thrown open for use as convalescent homes. The ambulance trains were not provided only by the LNWR; several companies seemed to have built them and they were used indiscriminately throughout the country. The bell code for ambulance trains was the same as for the Royal Train, 12 rings, 4-pause-4-pause-4.

One important special passenger train was put on for Naval personnel travelling between London and Scotland. It left Euston at 3pm in winter and 6pm in summer and was due past Oxenholme at 8.25pm and 11.25pm respectively. It had not been running long when the railwaymen christened it 'The Minesweeper'. Throughout the whole of the winter of 1917-18 it was worked nearly every night by

'Big Jumbo' No. 2186 *Lowther* in plain black livery about 1920.

Roger Carpenter collection

36

'Prince of Wales' No. 2396 *Queen of the Belgians*. Passing Oxenholme at 8.25pm it would be in Carlisle at 9.25pm in plenty of time for the engine to go on the shed, turn and be prepared again, and for the crew to have a rest, before returning to Crewe on the corresponding up train, which I understand was in Carlisle about midnight.

Sometimes 'The Minesweeper' was double-headed and if so its pilot was usually a Carlisle 'Precursor' that was working home. There were four or five 'Precursors' at Carlisle and among their regular duties were the vacuum-fitted express fish and meat trains that had to be in London for the early morning markets. They worked them as far as Crewe and if Crewe could not find a job for them to work back on, they would be sent back as assistant engine on 'The Minesweeper'. One night I remember it was double-headed by Carlisle 'Precursor' No. 2031 *Waverley*.

The Jellicoe Specials

By far the most important single wartime traffic was the movement of South Wales anthracite to Scotland, to the Firth of Forth and Scapa Flow, to supply the ships of the Royal Navy. This traffic was absolutely continuous for four and a half years. I have a copy of the Working Timetable for 1916, which was given to me by Jack Pinch, the signalman in No. 2 box. This covers the Lancaster & Carlisle district and shows there were seven loaded coal trains northbound and five empty trains southbound, passing through Oxenholme every day including Sundays. The loaded trains were made up of 40 wagons and a brake van and the empties of 56 wagons and a brake van. So the full and empty wagons balanced each other at 280 per day. This traffic was thus a continuous merry-go-round, and over the four and a half years it was in operation more than 11,000 of these trains passed through, carrying more than five million tons to Grangemouth from where it was transported by sea to Scapa Flow. The full trains were brought by the Great Western Railway to Chester, where the London & North Western Railway took over and conveyed them a further 137 miles to Carlisle. They passed right through Citadel station into Kingmoor yard where they were handed over to the Caledonian Railway.

These trains carried special telegraphing numbers on the front of the engine, the loaded trains proceeding north under 'P' series numbers, P1-100, and the trains of empty wagons returning south under 'C' numbers, C1-100. Both series started again when 100 had been reached, trains P100 and C100, for example, being followed by P1 and C1 respectively, and so on throughout the war until the traffic ceased.

The best engines for these coal trains were of course the 'Superheater Goods Class G1' 0-8-0s.

They handled them very easily but at times they were not available and then all kinds of engines were used from all kinds of sheds, and it must have been a very difficult job for the shedmaster at Chester to find suitable engines for these trains.

All these trains were banked from Oxenholme up the seven miles to Grayrigg and also again from Tebay up to Shap Summit. Special instructions were issued to the effect that no train was to ascend either of these banks unassisted in the rear even if there were two engines in front, so as to ease the strain on the couplings and to avoid any chance of a breakaway. Banking was done by '6ft 6in Jumbos' and they did a grand job. They did all the banking and hooking on in the early part of the war.

It was always fascinating to watch these trains, especially after they had stopped in the sidings south of the station and were restarting. The engines had to haul their train out of the siding and through the station unaided, because it was not possible to get the bank engine behind the guard's van alongside No. 2 signal box until the train had been drawn clear of the shed road. If a 'Super D' was at the front, it would start with no trouble and with its characteristic exhaust beat it would soon bring its train through the station. A 'B' class four-cylinder compound, however, would often have great difficulty in starting but the engines that had the greatest difficulty were the Whale '19in Goods' because being six-coupled engines they had less purchase on the rails. It was not easy for them to get a 750-ton train on the move, especially if the rails were wet, and sometimes it was necessary to send the bank engine right down to No. 1 signal box to get in behind the train and help it out.

About 1915-16 the shedmaster at Oxenholme, Mr Collins, was replaced by Mr Bunner, who came from Mold Junction in North Wales. Mr Bunner decided to try to get some 4-6-2 'Superheater Tanks' for banking purposes and he succeeded. A number of them were sent to Oxenholme and in 1916 three more came new from the works (Nos. 316, 2298 and 2384). The latter were actually sent for passenger work but the others were used on banking in preference to the 'Jumbos', which were then gradually reduced in number. Over the years all the class of 47 'Superheater Tanks' except for only three or four came to be shedded at either Oxenholme or Tebay at one time or another.

The men preferred the tank engines for several reasons. Being more powerful and having six coupled wheels instead of four, they were better suited to the heavy wartime traffic, when engines generally were in a worse state of repair and coal was often poor. They were also much more comfortable, because they had a rear spectacle plate which gave much better protection to the crew from the weather when running back light downhill. On the 'Jumbos'

'G1' class 0-8-0 No. 1121 at Upperby shed, Carlisle. It is specially reserved for use on Admiralty coal trains – hence the 'A' on the cab side as an indication that it should not be rostered to any other kind of work.

the men used to rig a tarpaulin from the front of the tender to the top of the cab to provide some shelter but it was scanty indeed in the rough and cold conditions that commonly occurred in the Fells, especially during winter.

After a while, because of the problem of finding suitable engines to work these trains, a number of 'Super Ds' were specially allocated for the coal traffic and carried a letter 'A' on a board hooked over the cabside above the numberplate on either side. This meant that the engine was reserved for the Admiralty coal trains and was an indication to the traffic people that they were not to be appropriated for any other work. Engines that were so noted were Nos. 1107, 1435, 1657 and 2258, all of which were stationed at Shed 19, Chester, and 1121, which was stationed at Shed 29, Carlisle.

As the war dragged on, many of the engines got into a poor state of repair and on Monday 15th April 1918 an instruction came into effect that trains were to be banked from Milnthorpe, six miles south of Oxenholme, for the full thirteen miles through to Grayrigg. The reason for this was to reduce delays by helping trains from the point where the serious climbing to Shap started and not just from Oxenholme. In addition, if the road was clear and the train engine did not need to stop at Oxenholme for water, they could get up speed before Oxenholme and so did not have to start the climb to Grayrigg from a dead stand.

The table below contains details of observations of some of these trains at Oxenholme. From the telegraphing numbers it is possible to calculate the total number of these trains which ran during the period of the observations. The table also shows the variety of engine classes that were used and the variety of sheds from which the engines came, and well illustrates the problem which the Locomotive Department faced in finding enough suitable engines for this traffic. Among the engines the greatest surprise is the combination of a '6ft Jumbo' and a 'Special DX' on a northbound train on 13th May 1918; they were probably put on at Preston as a result of the failure of the rostered engine from Chester. It is also clear that Oxenholme could not always find 'Superheater Tanks' for banking and would then use anything that was on hand. So on occasion they used an '18in Goods' and a '5ft 6in 2-4-2 Tank' and borrowed a Longsight 'Jumbo'.

'Jellicoe Specials' Observed at Oxenholme 1918-1919

Northbound Trains - Loaded

Date	Telegraph No.	Class	Engine No.	Name	Shed No	Shed Name	Banker Class	No.	Name	Shed No.	Name
24.2.1918	P41	'G1'	107		19	Chester	'6ft 6in'	1527	*Raleigh*	28º	Oxenholme
24.2.1918	P30	'G1'	674		19	Chester	'6ft 6in'	2176	*Robert Benson*	16	Longsight
2.3.1918		'G1'	1528		29	Carlisle	4-6-2T	1688		28º	Oxenholme
9.3.1918		'19in'	2615		16	Stockport	4-6-2T	1688		28º	Oxenholme
23.6.1918	P+0	'G1'	2290		29	Carlisle	4-6-2T	1688		28º	Oxenholme
23.6.1918		'G'	1789		19	Chester	4-6-2T	1184		28º	Oxenholme
23.6.1918	P16	'Exp'	1995	*Tornado*	27ᶜ	Carnforth	4-6-2T	1688		28º	Oxenholme
23.6.1918		'Exp'	2052	*Stephenson*	29	Carlisle	4-6-2T	1184		28º	Oxenholme
6.4.1918	P29	'D'	2527		19	Chester	4-6-2T	2384		28º	Oxenholme
6.4.1918	P30	'G1'	943		29	Carlisle					
20.4.1918	P43	-	-		-	-	4-6-2T	1533		28º	Oxenholme
20.4.1918	P39	'19in'	1126		15	Crewe South	4-6-2T	316		28º	Oxenholme
20.4.1918	P45	'G1'	107		19	Chester	4-6-2T	2298		28º	Oxenholme
24.4.1918		'19in'	1770		34	Patricroft	4-6-2T	316		28º	Oxenholme
24.4.1918	P77	'D'	1822		17	Leeds	4-6-2T	316		28º	Oxenholme
27.4.1918	P15	'G1'	943		29	Carlisle	4-6-2T	2298		28º	Oxenholme
27.4.1918	P11	'19in'	1544		25	Wigan	4-6-2T	2298		28º	Oxenholme
27.4.1918	P16	'G1'	2274		29	Carlisle	4-6-2T	1533		28º	Oxenholme
27.4.1918	P19 ⎰	'6ft 6in'	864	*Pilot*	29	Carlisle	4-6-2T	2298		28º	Oxenholme
	⎱	'G'	1647		19	Chester					
2.5.1918	P37	'D'	2527		19	Chester	4-6-2T	316		28º	Oxenholme
4.5.1918	P78	'D'	2526		25	Wigan	4-6-2T	316		28º	Oxenholme
4.5.1918	P89	'19in'	1656		34	Patricroft	4-6-2T	1533		28º	Oxenholme
6.5.1918	P94	'G1'	83		29	Carlisle	4-6-2T	1533		28º	Oxenholme
10.5.1918	P1	'G1'	720		29	Carlisle	4-6-2T	1533		28º	Oxenholme
11.5.1918	P35	'19in'	2508		15	Crewe South	4-6-2T	1533		28º	Oxenholme
11.5.1918	P39	'G1'	83		29	Carlisle	'18in'	473		28º	Oxenholme
11.5.1918	P41	'G1'	943		29	Carlisle	4-6-2T	1184		28º	Oxenholme
13.5.1918	P55 ⎰	'6ft'	1166	*Wyre*							
	⎱	'SDX'	3085								
31.8.1918	P78	'G1'	230		19	Chester	'5ft 6in'	466		28º	Oxenholme
31.8.1918	P89	'G1'	264		19	Chester	'6ft 6in'	1668	*Dagmar*	28º	Oxenholme
31.8.1918	P91	'G1'	83		29	Carlisle	4-6-2T	2298		28º	Oxenholme
16.11.1918	P70	'G1'	A1657		19	Chester	'6ft 6in'	1668	*Dagmar*	28º	Oxenholme
18.11.1918	P98	'G1'	A1121		29	Carlisle					
25.1.1919	P46	'D'	2530		27ᶜ	Carnforth	4-6-2T	2669		28º	Oxenholme

Southbound Trains - Empty

Date	Telegraph No.	Class	Engine No.	Name	Shed No	Shed Name
6.3.1918	C18	'19in'	2188		25	Wigan
6.3.1918	C19	'D'	1866		27	Carnforth
20.3.1918	C34	'Prince'	362	*Robert Southey*	15	Crewe
23.3.1918		'19in'	1998			Liverpool
27.3.1918	C8	'B'	2557		25	Wigan
27.3.1918	C9	'G'	508		16	Stockport
30.3.1918		'G1'	2274		29	Carlisle
30.3.1918		'Exp'	1603	*Princess Alexandra*	25	Wigan
30.3.1918		'G1'	83		29	Carlisle
2.5.1918	C36	'19in'	2229			Liverpool
6.5.1918	C51	'G1'	1121		29	Carlisle
6.5.1918	C52	'19in'	254		27	Preston
6.5.1918	C53	'Exp'	291	*Leander*	29	Carlisle
6.5.1918	C54	'19in'	939		15	Crewe
11.5.1918	C73	'D'	1857		25	Wigan
11.5.1918	C74	'D'				
31.8.1918	C27	'G1'	360		25	Wigan
18.11.1918	C97	'G1'	A1435		19	Chester

Abbreviations for engine classes

'18in'	'18in Goods' 0-6-0
'19in'	'19in Goods' 4-6-0
'5ft 6in'	'5ft 6in 2-4-2 Tank'
'6ft'	'6ft Jumbo' 2-4-0
'6ft 6in'	'6ft 6in Jumbo' 2-4-0
4-6-2T	'Superheater Tank' 4-6-2
'Exp'	'Experiment' class 4-6-0
'B'	'B' class four-cylinder compund 0-8-0
'D'	'D' class 0-8-0
'G'	'G' class 0-8-0
'G1'	'Superheater Goods Class G1' 0-8-0
'Prince'	'Prince of Wales' class 4-6-0
'SDX'	'Special DX' class 0-6-0

Other War Traffic

From time to time during the war exceptional workings took place. One afternoon a short train arrived headed by 'Prince of Wales' No. 362 *Robert Southey*. It consisted of a long low-loader wagon conveying a gun, which was reputed to weigh 81 tons, for the Fleet in Scotland and a brake van. In fact, when I arrived at the station, it was standing in the siding. Apparently, the driver, fireman and guard were time-expired (they had completed the maximum number of hours they were allowed to be on duty). Oxenholme men relieved them, the driver being Jack Docker, and took the train on to Carlisle. This was probably about 1916, as I remember an up passenger train the same afternoon was worked by one of the North British 'Princes' which were built in 1915, No. 446 *Pegasus*.

As the war went on, the strain it imposed on the Locomotive Department was enormous and it was then that all sorts of foreign engines from all over the line appeared on all kinds of special trains. I recall seeing two 'Bill Baileys' on such workings, Nos. 695 and 1113, and of course the Whale '19in Goods' 4-6-0s were to be seen every day. They did a lot of very good work on express goods trains, but so far as I am aware neither of these two classes was ever stationed at Oxenholme.

Mishaps

From time to time accidents and mishaps of various kinds occurred. In 1911 one of the new non-superheated 4-6-2 tank engines, of which twelve were built, was sent to Oxenholme, No. 1416. One day it had worked a train into Windermere and was being turned on the turntable there when it ran off the

'Prince of Wales' No. 362 *Robert Southey,* climbing away from Oxenholme with an 81-ton gun bound for the Royal Navy in Scotland. The driver is Geoff Docker of Oxenholme. I first saw this train waiting in the siding at Oxenholme in the morning but it did not leave until the afternoon. The mail pick up apparatus is some 100 yards behind the camera. *W. L. Harris*

table and down the embankment. It took four or five engines to pull it back. After it had been pulled back, it must have been sent to Crewe as it disappeared from the area. No more engines of the type were sent to Oxenholme until August 1912 when No. 932, one of the superheated engines, arrived new from the works. The intention seems to have been that it would work the short turn to Preston in the top link. If this had been done, it would have had to work the job every day, but the top-link men had always been used to keeping their own engine, no matter which turn they had been working. So it seems they opposed the idea and the engine was transferred to Crewe North.

On another occasion 'Prince of Wales' No. 2249 *Thomas Campbell* suffered a major failure. One day in 1917 I was standing on the down platform directly opposite the telegraph office on the up platform when Mr Bunner came out of the office. He saw me and came straight across to the edge of the platform and said, 'I've got something very interesting for you at the shed. Come on down with me.' Mr Bunner was always very friendly towards me and liked to tell me what he was doing and what was going on. In this respect, he was quite a contrast to Mr Collins, his predecessor, who would not have anybody in or near the shed. Anyway, I turned and walked to the south end of the platform while he walked to the end of the up platform and then crossed the tracks to join me and walk down to the shed.

It turned out that the 'Prince' had broken its crank axle when rounding the curve in the deep rock cutting at Hay Fell. They had managed to get the engine down to Oxenholme but the shed there was not equipped to remove the driving wheels. So they had had to fasten them up in such a way that they were clear of the rails in order to send the engine for repair to Carlisle. He had dismantled the motion and coupling rods and placed them in the tender, after first removing the coal, and had taken the brasses out of the crank-axle bearings. Then he had put tie rods through the wheels from one side to the other, with screw nuts on the ends, and a plate at each side, and had pulled the whole contraption tight, so that the broken parts of the crank axle fitted together and could not move. He then hung brackets on the footplating and after jacking the axle up, he secured it to the brackets in such a way that it was suspended from the footplate with the wheels about 4in above the rails.

This had already been done when I saw it in the shed. As I was there 4-6-2 'Superheater Tank' No. 327 arrived from Tebay with a brake van. An Oxenholme engine took the brake van and pushed it into the shed. The 'Prince' was facing south and the van was coupled up to it. It was then pulled back out of the shed and pushed up on to the 'Superheater Tank'. The couplings were fastened and away the crippled 'Prince' went to Carlisle.

One of Mr Whale's '19in Goods' 4-6-0s in LMS days. These engines did an enormous amount of hard work during the First World War.

Leaving School

I left school at Christmas 1915 and went to work in the woollen mill in Kendal. I had been hoping to leave at Easter 1916 as I was captain of the football team and wanted to complete the season but my father decided that I should leave and start work. Because of my interest in the LNWR and its locomotives, I would have liked to have gone to Crewe to become an apprentice in the Locomotive Department but I have no regrets that things did not work out that way.

As we entered 1918, the war was still dragging on and I knew I would be called up to join the Army on my eighteenth birthday along with all the other boys of that age. Sure enough, my call up papers arrived on 13th April. I was instructed to report to the Head Quarters of the Border Regiment at Carlisle Castle on 13th May. We all had this one month's notice.

Travelling to Carlisle that day, I reached the castle in the late morning and with the lads of my age was duly enrolled in the 4th Border Regiment. We stayed in the castle for a few days, presumably till our numbers had grown sufficiently, and were then taken by train to Filey on the Yorkshire coast. From there we marched to Hunmanby, where we found ourselves in camp in bell tents.

Our programme of fourteen weeks intensive training started immediately the next day and covered every branch of infantry warfare. The training was continuous from Monday to Friday and the physical and mental effort tested everyone to the limit. Sometimes we had battalion manoeuvres in the afternoon with a junior officer in charge and sometimes he got tied up in knots. Then it was hard on us while he got things sorted out.

On Saturday we went on a five-mile route march around the countryside with the band in front. We carried full pack and had a ten-minute break on the roadside every hour. That suited me fine. I could have gone on all day. On Sunday morning we had a church service on the parade ground. Saturday and Sunday afternoons were free and we could go down to the village of Hunmanby or walk to Filey.

My army training continued till early in August 1918. When we were supposed to be proficient in everything, we – that is, three and four platoons – were sent home on a week's draft leave before leaving for France. Lloyd George had said, however, that he would stop sending the boys to France when 'the tide turned'. It so happened that it 'turned' at Cambrai while we were on leave and when we returned to camp, we found that our draft had been cancelled. After the way we had been worked up, the anti-climax was terrific and took some adjusting to. There seemed to be no reality in anything.

Anyway, we stayed in camp at Hunmanby till October, when we marched the thirteen miles to Bridlington where we were billetted in empty houses. A demobilisation officer was appointed and those who had any special reason for leaving were allowed to go.

I came home on 1st January 1919 and went back to my work in the mill. In due course I served my time there and went through all the various departments, eventually finishing up in the office on the management side. The mill was engaged in woollen manufacture and did every process, from the raw wool to the finished cloth. Among the many things we made were blankets and rugs for railway sleeping cars on the London & North Western Railway, the Midland Railway and several other railways, and also for the liners and ships, P&O, Cunard and so on. There was also a horse-clothing department, which made up blankets and sheets, and also the leather-work, for the wholesale trade. It was quite a thriving business, especially during the war, but it went down in the slump during the 1930s and my life then went in other directions.

In 1919 my family moved to Windermere and while I was living there, I fell in love with the Lake District. During the 1920s and 1930s I walked the valleys and climbed the mountains and I know it all intimately. I have seen it in all weathers, in all conditions and at all times of year. It must surely by the most beautiful area in the whole of England.

Post-war Railway Memories

From Windermere I travelled to Kendal and back every day by train, of course, as there was no other means of transport. We started work at 8am then and I used to catch a train from Windermere just after 7am. After a while, when I got up into the office, I started later and so went down on the 'Club Train' at 8.30am. Later still I used to go at the same time as my father on the 8.40am stopping train which went through to Grange-over-Sands. We got into the office at about 8.55am; it was only about 7 or 8 minutes walk from the station.

I used to come back on the 6.34 in the evening, as we finished at 6pm. That was the return working of the 'Club Train'. One night it went out at 6.32 and so I quibbled with the foreman. 'Oh, well' he said, 'it's 6.32 into here. You're supposed to be here at 6.32. We have a right to send it out at 6.32.' Anyway, I didn't really care. I used to go across the line and sit on a bench and watch them playing cricket.

If I was kept late for any reason, I could always go on the 7.1pm, which was the 5.5pm from Manchester to Windermere. It was a faster train, as it only called at Preston, Lancaster and Kendal, and was due in

Windermere about 7.19. It ran straight through the main-line platform at Oxenholme without stopping but of course at much reduced speed so that it could take the branch.

Occasionally I have seen a railwayman 'jump' it. He would jump on to the footboard of a carriage as it ran through, open the door and swing himself in. Of course, he had to start well down the platform to give himself time to get the door closed before the water column at the end of the platform. It was a tempting thing to do as it would save him a bit of time not having to wait for a train stopping at Oxenholme but it was foolish as well. If he had made a mistake, he could easily have been killed.

One day in the late 1920s I went to Manchester for the day and used this train to return to Kendal. At the time it was worked by Wigan men and was routed by the Whelley line, which joined the LNWR main line at Standish Junction. They used engines of the 'Prince of Wales' class, LMS Nos 5809-16, which were shedded at Wigan. The driver was driving by the regulator (which means he kept the engine in full forward gear and controlled the speed by adjusting the regulator opening) and so the 'Prince' thumped its way along all the way to Kendal. With only a light train and driven expansively (with the regulator wide and early cut-off of steam in the cylinders), the engine would have run silently. It really was dreadful to hear it and I wished I could have had the chance to alter it.

Not knowing the Windermere branch, the Wigan men had a pilot, officially from Oxenholme but in this case from Kendal. Arriving there, I saw the pilot was a young fireman who I knew quite well, though I never knew his name. He had recently passed as a driver and was a very keen young man who was anxious to learn all he could about engines and about driving them. He told me he attended all the improvement classes which were held at Carnforth.

He always drove expansively, and what a transformation there was when we left Kendal! The engine was now to all intents inaudible. We passed Burneside at a rare speed and sailed up the bank through Staveley to Black Moss in record time. Then our young man made a mistake down the mile long bank into Windermere. He reached for the brake too late and we were going so fast when we took the crossover into No. 2 platform that I thought we would jump the track. Fortunately we did not but in order to stop before the buffers he had to reverse the engine and we stopped very quickly, quite a way from the buffers as it happened. Reversing is a very effective way of stopping in a hurry but it does not do the engine any good. Our young driver had misjudged his braking completely but luckily had managed to get away with it. I gave him a look but even when I

saw him later I never mentioned the way he had stopped, though I knew what had happened and he knew I knew.

Although Kendal was only on the branch, it was quite interesting waiting for my train there in the evening as there was always something to see. There was a driver I knew very well, Tom Nelson, who often used to be waiting with his 'Superheater Tank' by the carriage shed, just off the north end of the southbound platform. I was on the northbound platform, of course, but I used to go across and get up on the engine and chat to him while I was waiting for my train. Unfortunately, I never asked him what working brought him there but his job was to bank the 6.40pm goods from Kendal to Oxenholme.

Kendal yard was quite interesting as the wagons ran down into the sidings by gravity – the engineers had laid it out so as to use the natural slope of the land in this way. The yard was normally shunted by an Oxenholme '18in Goods'. When the 6.40pm goods arrived from Windermere, after picking up wagons at Staveley and Burneside, it reversed on to the down line and then drew forward and entered the yard with the engine at the Oxenholme end. The '18in Goods' then added the Kendal wagons and did whatever shunting was needed to put all the wagons in their correct positions in the train. When the train was made up, the train engine backed it out on the down line and then came forward on the up line through the platform. After it had cleared the points by the carriage shed, the signalmen moved them over and let the 4-6-2 tank, which was running bunker-first (facing Windermere, that is), back on to the rear of the train. Then away they would go up the two miles of 1 in 96 to Oxenholme. The '18in Goods' returned to Oxenholme light engine later.

One evening in August 1919 I was waiting on the station at Kendal for my usual 6.32pm train home to Windermere when I noticed the afternoon goods was ready marshalled for departure to Oxenholme, headed by a four-cylinder compound 0-8-0 goods engine that had the number 3406 in large figures on its tender. As I was in plenty of time, I left the platform and went down into the yard to have a closer look. The engine was No. 41 and the shed-plate 35 told me it belonged to Speke Junction and was probably on loan. The 2500-gallon tender, No. 635, had been overseas during the war attached to the '17in Coal Engine' 0-6-0 numbered 3406 in the LNWR duplicate list. It was the practice of the Railway Operating Division to display the engine number in large figures on the tender. In this case the tender must have come from one of the engines which were returned from France after the war. The compound goods No. 41 was rebuilt in August 1921 as a 'Superheater Goods'. I remember seeing it in rebuilt condition one day just outside Carlisle.

Interior of Windermere station looking along platform 2, with Wyman's bookstall on the left. This platform was used by all main-line trains both arriving and departing.

Bernard Matthews collection

Having moved to Windermere, I saw less of Oxenholme but I still kept in touch with what was going on in different ways. In the evening I often used to walk up to Windermere station to meet the last train in at 9.40pm. Every third week Tom Nelson used to work this train and I used to get up on the footplate for a chat till he got the signal to back out the empty coaches. I had just got down on to the platform one evening when Mr Graham the stationmaster came across the platform to me. He said he had noticed I appeared to be taking an interest in everything and if I liked I could have his permission to go anywhere at my own risk. I said I would like to have his permission and thanked him. Thereafter I used to stay on the footplate till the driver was ready to depart for Oxenholme.

The main interest in meeting the last train was because the engine that worked it was not only not an Oxenholme engine but could come from any shed and was different every night. For some reason I never enquired why this was. On the evening of 2nd August 1926, the train was worked by 'Rebuilt Precursor' No. 7 *Titan*, which I had never seen before either before or after rebuilding. It was then shedded at Shed 26, Edge Hill, Liverpool. I had no sooner got on the footplate when Tom said, 'This is a grand engine. I think I'll ask our boss if he will try to keep it'. I told him there was not a chance, as it was too well known up and down the line. All the engines of a class were not equally good. Before being rebuilt this one had run trials between Rugby and Brighton against a London Brighton & South Coast Railway 'I3' class superheated 4-4-2 tank. The latter had been proved far superior in coal and water consumption and led to the development of the superheated 'George the Fifth' class at Crewe.

I always knew I could drive a North Western engine, if I got the chance, and it was about this time

that the chance came – in the General Strike of 1926. On the first day of the strike I cycled the nine miles to Kendal in the morning and after work rode to Oxenholme to find out what was happening. When I arrived, I found a three-coach train on the point of leaving for Windermere. Mr Bunner, the Oxenholme shedmaster, was in charge of the engine. He had with him two young men who were students in the Engineering Department of Liverpool University. They were to be in charge of the engine the following day.

I put my cycle in the van and climbed up with them. The engine was a 'Superheater Tank', previously LNWR No. 1533 but now numbered 6978 by the LMS. The cab was quite full with four of us but off we went down to Kendal and then on through Burneside and Staveley to Windermere with Mr Bunner driving all the way. Having learnt that the two students would be working my 8.40am train in the morning, I bade them all farewell and rode home.

The 8.40am train was a local, stopping at all stations to Grange-over-Sands via Oxenholme, Hincaster Junction and Arnside. It was not long before I thought that if two students could work it, so could I, at least as far as Kendal. Having done the journey every day for some years, I knew exactly where the engine needed steam and where to apply the brakes. So without saying anything to anyone, I thought it all out during the evening.

The next morning when I walked up to the station as usual, instead of entering number 2 platform, I went along number 3 and arrived alongside the turntable and water column where the engine was already standing. It had been turned, which in a way was better for me as I had not visualised running bunker first. I said 'Good morning' to the students and then 'I'll take her down this morning', and climbing

The 'Superheater Tank' which I drove from Windermere to Kendal in the General Strike, No. 6978. It is seen here south of Lancaster with a 13-coach up express. The first vehicle is a double-ended slip coach.

on to the engine took my place on the driver's side. I had a few words with them about how they were getting on and then when the signal was pulled off, I took the engine out of the siding on to the main line. I then backed down on to the train and one of the students coupled up. When I got the right away from the guard, I opened the regulator and we were off.

On leaving the station, the line rises at about 1 in 80 for nearly a mile to Black Moss. Then after passing under a bridge, it falls at about the same gradient to Staveley and there the engine would run more or less without steam. I knew exactly where to shut off and apply the brakes, and so made a normal stop at Staveley station. Then off we went again, over the level crossing on the Kendal to Windermere road and still on the falling gradient we passed under Plantation Bridge and so down to Burneside where we again made a normal stop at the platform.

From Burneside to Kendal the distance is two miles with the first one rising slightly and the second falling. We negotiated this without any difficulty and having told the students it was all theirs again, I wished them farewell and climbed down on to the platform. I was told I had made a 'normal' run.

Under strike conditions, any engine that was available was used to work any train that could be run. In the 1919 strike, for instance, this same train from Windermere was once worked by 'Prince of Wales' No. 2213 *Charles Kingsley* of Shed 17, Leeds, and on another occasion by 'Big Jumbo' No. 506 *Sir Alexander Cockburn*, which was also a stranger. I had never seen either of these engines before and I never saw them again.

Where the engine I drove in 1926, No. 6978, came from I am not sure, though it may have been Tebay, but certainly all the Oxenholme 'Superheater Tanks'

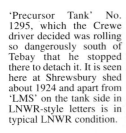

'Precursor Tank' No. 1295, which the Crewe driver decided was rolling so dangerously south of Tebay that he stopped there to detach it. It is seen here at Shrewsbury shed about 1924 and apart from 'LMS' on the tank side in LNWR-style letters is in typical LNWR condition.

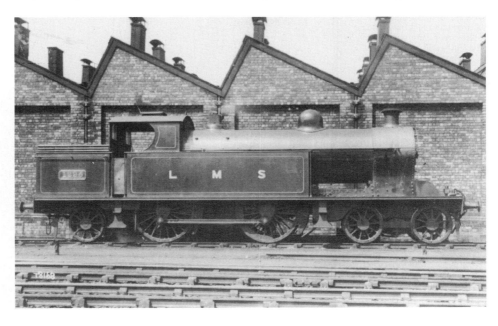

45

were sent to Buxton early in 1921 in exchange for 'Precursor Tanks'. Presumably, the extra power of the 4-6-2 tanks was more useful with passenger trains on the banks between Manchester and Buxton. With the reduction in traffic, the 'Precursor Tanks' were adequate for banking and thanks to their bigger driving wheels were better suited to fast running when hooked on to the front of an express. The 'Precursor Tanks' received from Buxton were: Nos 762, 803, 1164, 1219, 1295, 1356 and 1551.

One day in the early 1920s 'Precursor Tank' No. 1295 hooked on to one of the night sleepers worked by a Crewe man. All went well on the climb to Grayrigg but when the train picked up speed on the level beyond Low Gill the Crewe man became alarmed at the way the 'Precursor Tank' rolled about. So after taking water at Dillicar Troughs, he braked hard and stopped the train in Tebay station. He said he would not go any further with an engine rolling so dangerously in front of him; he would report it to Crewe and take a banker from Tebay instead. So the Oxenholme men had to hook off.

The Oxenholme driver was Jim Duxbury and he told me later that he had not been at all worried since he was used to the way the engine rolled and knew that though it was uncomfortable it was safe. In any case, the Crewe man had made an error of judgement in stopping his train. As the climbing starts immediately after Tebay station, the speed of the train would soon have been reduced and with it the rolling of his assisting engine. As it was, time was wasted detaching the pilot and taking a banker from Tebay.

After the war Oxenholme received its first members of the 'Prince of Wales' class. They were transferred from other sheds and were invariably in run down condition and ready for overhaul at Crewe. One of them was No. 525 *Vulcan* and one of my driver friends, Tom Nelson, said it was in a shocking state. It was just an example of the arrears of maintenance work which had built up during the war.

The first newly overhauled 'Prince' to be shedded at Oxenholme was No. 173 *Livingstone*, which arrived late in 1922, after full repainting had been resumed. It was a picture. For the races at Aintree in March 1922 an instruction was issued that all special trains were to be worked by newly painted engines, and so No. 173 was sent to Carlisle on loan for the day.

The first new 'Princes' to be sent straight to Oxenholme were Nos. 240, 243 and 274, which were delivered by the firm of William Beardmore in 1921. After the LMS had introduced its block numbering allocation of engines four of the class were shedded at Oxenholme with the instruction that one was always to be kept standing in steam to deal with any emergency. These four were Nos. 148, 224, 227 and 232, which then had LMS numbers 5764-7. Since No. 5765 was inclined to run hot, it got the job of stand-by and it used to stand alongside the shed by the main line where it was easily available if needed.

In May 1925 the LMS held some engine trials between Preston and Carlisle. The engines tested were 'Prince of Wales' No. 90 *Kestrel*, 'Claughton' No. 30 *Thalaba*, Midland compound No. 1065 and Lancashire & Yorkshire Railway 4-6-0 LMS No. 10460. The LNWR engines were in charge of drivers W. J. Scott and J. Westwood of Carlisle respectively, the Midland engine had Midland men and the L&Y engine L&Y men. The test lasted for a fortnight. Afterwards Derby considered that the compound was better than the 'Prince' and flooded the LMS with more of them but the 'Claughton' was better than the L&Y 4-6-0 and lighter on coal. In later years it was recognised that the two LNWR engines were the best.

These three drivers are standing on the bridge carrying the Kendal to Kirkby Lonsdale Road over the main line adjacent to Oxenholme No. 1 signal box in May 1925. The driver on the right, who was then retired, is Jack Thornborough. The one on the left leaning on the bridge is his son, Frank, who at that time was in the extra link. The driver in the middle is the first driver I ever spoke to, Jack Speed. When I first knew him in 1911, he was one of the top-link drivers, his engine being No. 374 *Empress*. At the time the photograph was taken he was in the 'old man's link' and used to work between Windermere and Grange-over-Sands on the Furness line. He once told me that he was at Grange-over-Sands soon after the Grouping when a Furness man called to him, 'How do you like it since we took you over?' He seemed incensed by the remark!

A double-headed Glasgow-Euston express running into Preston in May 1925. Both engines still have their pre-grouping numbers, LNWR 'Experiment' No. 1781 *Lightning* and L&YR 'Dreadnought' No. 1662.

F. Dean collection

'19in Goods' class 4-6-0 No. 1613 climbing the 1 in 98 bank southwards from Lancaster with an up goods. Most probably a banker is hard at work out of sight at the rear of the train.

H. Gordon Tidey

The 'Prince of Wales' class did a lot of very good work in those years. Although I lived in Windermere then, I still used to keep in touch by going to Oxenholme and sometimes further afield. Occasionally I went to Preston by train on a Saturday afternoon and returned on the 'Second Corridor', as we called it, which left Preston at 6.40pm and which in the late 1920s was often hauled by a large-boilered 'Claughton' such as No. 2499 *Patience*.

One particular occasion I remember illustrates what grand men and grand engines the London & North Western Railway used to have. I was on the station at Preston on 8th August 1930, when I saw a Beardmore 'Prince', LMS No. 5764, previously LNWR No. 148, arrive with the 4.25pm from Windermere. The load was 18 carriages. A number of coaches had probably come off the Furness line and been added at Carnforth. I recognised the driver as Frank Thornborough – he was a grand chap and a grand driver – but unfortunately I was standing on the big island platform and as he came in on the East Lancashire line, I could not speak to him then because there were two sets of metals between us.

Anyhow, some weeks later Frank was working the 8.40am stopping train from Windermere to Grange on which I used to travel down to Kendal. So I was able to ask him about the trip.

'Good morning, Frank.'

'Good morning.'

'Can you cast your mind back to August Bank Holiday? I was on the island platform at Preston when you came in with the 4.25pm from Windermere. Can you tell me what weight you had on?'

He nodded and said, '483 tons'.

'That was some train. It would be about 520 tons loaded.'

'Oh, yes. It was all of that.'

Trains leaving Lancaster for the south are faced with a bank one mile long at 1 in 98 up to Lancaster No. 1. So I said, 'I suppose you had a bank engine up to No. 1 signal box at Lancaster.'

'No, there wasn't one available.'

'Well then, how did you get on?'

'Oh, all right. She's a grand strong engine, that one. I just got her quietly on the move and then opened her right out, and we went up in fine style.'

'I wish I could have heard it. How long did you take to Preston?'

'We're allowed 26 minutes. I took 27.'

'I reckon that was good going. I'd better get in. The guard's waving his flag.'

So he had climbed the bank out of Lancaster without the help of a bank engine and had still only taken 27 minutes for the 21 miles from there to Preston.

On another occasion sometime later in the 1930s when I was talking to Frank, he told me that one day when he was returning from Shap Summit and approaching Scout Green, he could see a long passenger train had been stopped by signal on the 1 in 75 gradient with no bank engine behind. He also saw his signal was at red, so he stopped alongside the train engine, a Stanier Pacific, as he wanted to see how the driver (with whom he no doubt exchanged a few words) managed to start the train without running back. The Crewe driver's signal cleared first, so Frank was able to watch. He first opened the regulator enough for the steam pressure in the cylinders to hold the train while the brakes were coming off. He then started to blow them off and as they came off he opened the regulator further and further. In that way he got the train moving without the slightest sign of it running back or of the engine slipping. This was a wonderful example of driving expertise and Frank was full of admiration for the Crewe driver's skill. He was a fine driver himself, yet recognised and respected another expert when he saw one.

Epilogue

When I was a boy, Oxenholme always had plenty to maintain my interest and was a wonderful place to learn about engines. When the expresses had gone, there was always something to watch, the goods trains, the branch train to Windermere, the shunting in the yard and the activity of the bankers which were used to help trains up to Grayrigg or right through to Shap Summit.

In the early 1930s my interest remained as strong as ever but the mill where I worked began to suffer from the depression and after a time was closed. So I decided to leave the area to seek work further south and eventually settled in a country district in the Midlands.

Throughout my life I have had two main interests, the locomotives of the London & North Western Railway and the Lake District. These two interests have helped me greatly whenever I have been worried about life's problems. I have always lived in or near the country and feel I belong to the country. I also feel the longer one lives in the country, the more one feels there is something far bigger than we are which pervades everything.

Un-named 'Claughton' No. 8 on an up express climbing the bank south of Lancaster. The rear of the train is just passing Lancaster No. 1 signal box and the banker, which appears to be a '17in Coal Engine', is just dropping off the back of the train. In the loop on the far right an up goods waits to follow once the section is clear.